PLATE I

STELA OF ROMA

A SYRIAN SETTLER IN EGYPT ABOUT B.C. 1200. HIS LEG SHOWS THE TYPICAL DEFORMATION
RESULTING FROM INFANTILE PARALYSIS

Copenhagen Museum

MAGICIAN AND LEECH

A STUDY IN THE BEGINNINGS OF MEDICINE WITH SPECIAL REFERENCE TO ANCIENT EGYPT

BY

WARREN R. DAWSON, F.R.S.E.

FELLOW OF THE ROYAL SOCIETY OF MEDICINE

WITH SIX ILLUSTRATIONS

PREFACE

SOME years ago I began a systematic study of the Egyptian medical texts with the optimistic intention of translating them. After working through the material (the extent of which is indicated in Chapter V), I soon came to the conclusion that a complete translation was an impossibility. In the first place, most of the texts are very corrupt, and some are full of blunders; all are written in an idiomatic and specialized style; and last, but not least, they abound in technical terms for few of which we are able to find adequate equivalents. Some of the anatomical terms are still unknown, many of the pathological terms and names of diseases and the great majority of the drugs have not yet been accurately identified. Moreover, the Egyptian methods of expression would often require a long commentary to make them intelligible to readers unacquainted with the language. In spite, however, of their many difficulties and obscurities, the purport, if not the actual words, of the papyri are usually clear enough, and a prolonged study of the texts will enable the student to form a fair, if not a full, idea of the nature and extent of the medical knowledge of the ancient Egyptians. I have published, from time to time, in scientific journals, numerous communications dealing with the identity and history of a number of drugs and anatomical terms, with various aspects of Egyptian medical practice, and with the technique of mummification.

The results of my own studies have convinced me that most of the accounts of Egyptian medicine published in the various medical histories are unsatisfactory. They are for the most part based upon opinions expressed by Egyptologists many years ago, when our knowledge of the language was far less advanced than it is to-day, and before many of the documents now known had been discovered. It seems to me, also, that some of the historians have placed too much reliance upon premature translations that often do violence to grammar and syntax and are very largely composed of guess-work where the technical terms are concerned, for many diseases and drugs have been rashly identified in a manner that will not stand the test of critical examination. The result has been in most cases to give a false impression of the Egyptian concepts of sickness and disease and their treatment. To one translation in particular can be traced many of the erroneous statements that have been copied from book to book for the last fifty years.

Whilst we are still very far from being able to give a detailed account of Egyptian medicine, a careful study of the texts reveals the important part that Egypt has played in the development of science : the Egyptian papyri are the earliest medical documents that have survived, and they must necessarily form the starting-point of all studies of the history of medicine. For comparison, I have added a short chapter on Assyrian medicine.

Many colleagues and friends have urged me to publish an account of Egyptian medicine, and I have written this little book, which is no more than a brief summary of the contents of my note-books, in response to this oft-expressed desire. My aim has been, within a short compass, to trace the evolution of medicine from its parent magic, and I have based my statements upon a careful study of the texts themselves, and upon the examination of a large series of mummies, for the technique of mummification has had an important influence on the growth of anatomical knowledge.

The study of Egyptian medicine has involved a great deal of reading in the early medical literature of other countries, and this has often suggested the interpretation of obscure passages in the papyri and has revealed the extent to which other nations have borrowed Egyptian ideas and practices.

I would like to make it clear that although I have for years been keenly interested in the history of medicine and have written a number of memoirs on the subject, I am not a medical man. I mention this point because reviewers and reporters have often in the past credited me with medical diplomas that I do not possess.

To many medical friends I am indebted for advice and assistance in matters of anatomy, physiology and pathology ; and amongst these I would like especially to thank Professor G. Elliot Smith, F.R.S., with whom I have discussed these matters frequently both personally and by correspondence during the last twelve years ; to Dr. J. B. Hurry, M.D., I am indebted for much information ; and to Sir Arthur Keith,

F.R.S., I wish to express my gratitude for his kindness in allowing me access to the valuable material in the Museum of the Royal College of Surgeons.

W. R. D.

CONTENTS

LIST OF ILLUSTRATIONS

MAGICIAN AND LEECH

CHAPTER I

PRIMITIVE IDEAS ON LIFE, DISEASE AND DEATH

PRIMITIVE man was not an abstract thinker and long ages had elapsed before he had accumulated the concrete knowledge necessary to convince him that death is the inevitable fate of all living creatures. Even at the present time many peoples believe that life should endure indefinitely and that the state we call death is merely an altered form of living, a break in the daily routine of existence, brought about by some agency, human or supernatural, which the wits of the living can and must counteract. Death as the negation of life is an abstract concept which was entirely outside the mental powers of primitive man. To an individual there can be no such state as death, because it is a fate which befalls others and is never true of the individual himself, for as soon as he dies he cannot contemplate a state which only comes into being when his consciousness has fled.

Before any attempt can be made to study the history of human effort to prolong life and to avert extinction —an effort out of which the magician, the priest and the doctor had their origin—it is necessary to make

1

some preliminary inquiries into the ideas and concepts concerning disease and death which are held by primitive peoples to-day, and by those nations of antiquity whose records are intelligible to us.

A common concept regards death in general as an accidental liability that has not always existed, but was introduced on a particular occasion by revengeful gods or by some other circumstance. This belief is proved by the existence of many myths and traditions that have been framed to account for the origin of the phenomenon of death. There are many primitive peoples at the present day who attribute death to two causes only—violence and sorcery—and who believe that if men never died violent deaths and were never bewitched, they would be immortal and would live for ever.[1] Some Australian tribes, for instance, attribute death to physical violence or sorcery without which life would endure indefinitely.[2] This belief is typical of many, and numerous parallel instances could be quoted from Indonesia, Melanesia, America and elsewhere.[3] It will be observed that a distinction is made between natural death and violent death, a point to which we shall return.

[1] E. B. Tylor, *Primitive Culture*, ed. 2 (London 1873), Vol. i, p. 138.

[2] W. E. Roth, *Ethnological Studies among the North-West-Central Queensland Aborigines* (Brisbane 1897), p. 161.

[3] For references and instances, see J. G. Frazer, *The Golden Bough*, ed. 3; *The Dying God* (London 1911), pp. 1–2; E. Crawley, *The Mystic Rose* (ed. Besterman), Vol. i (London 1927), pp. 32 *sq.*; E. Crawley, art. ' Life and Death (Primitive) ' in *Hastings' Encyclopædia of Religion and Ethics*, Vol. viii (Edinburgh 1915), p. 9; W. H. R. Rivers, *Medicine, Magic and Religion* (London 1924), pp. 5 ff.

As already mentioned, there is a widespread belief that at one time there was no such thing as death, but that it came into existence at a definite time. According to some traditions, man lost the gift of immortality because he disobeyed the god or gods; according to others, this loss was brought about through the stupidity or malevolence of some animal. In this connection one may quote as examples two traditions that are held by the Wachagga, a Bantu people inhabiting the Kilimanjaro district of Africa. According to one of these traditions, which is almost identical with the Biblical story,[1] human mortality is the result of eating a certain fruit which the Great God had forbidden men to eat whilst he allowed them the full enjoyment of all other fruits. Death came into the world as man's punishment for disobedience. According to the other tradition, the god sent his messenger to inform mankind that they would enjoy a perpetual renewal of youth by casting their skins when old age approached. The god granted this boon on one condition, namely, that no eye should witness this act of sloughing. A certain old man, when his skin was partly cast, allowed himself to be seen by his grand-daughter, and as the result of his disobedience to the divine command, mankind lost for ever the gift of renewed youthfulness.[2] This legend is closely paralleled, although with certain variations, in many parts of the world. There is for instance a tradition in some of the Melanesian islands, that men lost the power of renewing youth

[1] *Genesis*, chs. ii and iii.
[2] C. Dundas, *Kilimanjaro and its People* (London 1924), pp. 108 *sq.*

2

by casting their skins because on one occasion an old woman, after sloughing, resumed her cast-off skin.[1] In other instances the boon which mankind had lost was believed to have been transferred to snakes and other reptiles who still enjoy the power of an annual renewal of youth. Variant versions of these traditions are found in many parts of the New and the Old Worlds.[2] Brief reference may also be made to the belief that death was brought into the world by certain animals. The natives of Portuguese East Africa, for instance, will not touch a chameleon (although they will handle other reptiles) because they believe that that animal first brought death into the world.[3] The origin of this tradition is probably similar to others in which it is supposed that reptiles had cheated man out of the power of renewing his youth in order to usurp that power themselves.[4]

The ideas concerning death held by the ancient Egyptians are full of perplexities and apparent inconsistencies. Of all the nations of antiquity, the Egyptians paid most attention to funerary matters. They took the most elaborate pains to secure the continuity of existence of the individual, and refused

[1] R. H. Codrington, *The Melanesians* (Oxford 1891), pp. 260, 265.

[2] A collection of examples with references will be found in J. G. Frazer, *The Golden Bough*, ed. 3 ; *The Scapegoat* (London 1913), pp. 302 *sq.* ; *Folk-Lore in the Old Testament* (London 1919), Vol. i, pp. 52–76.

[3] Mr. Hugh Cott, at a meeting of the Zoological Society of London on November 15th, 1927. For similar instances see J. G. Frazer, *Folk-Lore in the Old Testament* (London 1919), Vol. i, p. 57.

[4] Cf. J. G. Frazer, *loc. cit.*

to contemplate extinction. Yet they apparently
regarded death not as an accidental misfortune which
had invaded a previously immortal world, but as a
fact coeval with the creation of life itself. A passage
of the *Pyramid Texts* refers to a state 'when heaven
was not, when earth was not, when mankind was
not, before the gods were born, before death had
come into existence'.[1] This implies a belief that
death was created at the same time as the heavens,
the earth, the gods and mankind. Yet these same
texts repeatedly deny the fact of death, and the
dead king for whose benefit and upon the walls of
whose tomb they were inscribed, is continually spoken
of as living. Again and again we meet with such
expressions as these : ' Have ye said that he is dead ?
He dieth not ', ' Thou hast not come forth dead,
thou hast come forth living ', ' Thou hast come forth
that thou mightest live : thou hast come forth that
thou mightest not die '. In scores of similar phrases
the *Pyramid Texts* voice a passionate protest against
death.[2] The revolt against death finds expression in

---

[1] The *Pyramid Texts*, which we shall frequently have
occasion to quote in the course of this book, are the long
magical and funerary texts inscribed upon the walls of the
chambers in the pyramids of the Kings of the Fifth and Sixth
Dynasties (*circa* 2675–2475 B.C.). They constitute the oldest
body of religious texts in the world. The numbers quoted
are those of the sections into which the text has been divided
by Prof. K. Sethe in his edition, *Die altägyptische Pyramiden-
texte* (Leipsic 1908). The passage here quoted is § 1466, and
the translation is that of A. H. Gardiner, *Hastings' Encyclopædia of Religion and Ethics*, Vol. viii (Edinburgh 1915), p. 24.

[2] *Pyramid Texts*, §§ 134, 350, 657, 775, 781, 792, 810, 833,
867, 875, 1262, 1453, 1464, 1477, 1810, 1812, 1975, 2201, etc.

Egyptian texts in another way, that is by the frequent and deliberate avoidance of the use of the words 'death' and 'dead', and by employing euphemisms instead. The dead are often called 'those who are yonder', or 'the weary ones', and death may be spoken of as 'putting into port', 'attaining blessedness', or 'passing away', a phrase in common use to-day. The king's name, throughout the historic period of Egypt, is usually followed by the words 'endowed, like Rē, with life for ever', and the Pharaoh, who when alive is called 'the good god', is styled when dead, not 'the dead god', but 'the great god'.[1]

In spite of all that has been said to the contrary in innumerable books on the religious ideas of the Egyptians, it is more than doubtful if they had any fundamental belief in immortality in a spiritual sense. We shall return to this point in a later chapter, and shall discuss the evidence which seems to point to the fact that the underlying belief was not, originally at least, a belief in the immortality of the soul, but an age-long endeavour to secure the continuity of physical life.

The Egyptians had another conception regarding death. They believed not only in the 'breath of life', but also in the 'breath of death'. Air was as essential to the dead as to the living, and again and again in funerary texts, the dead man uses spells in order to procure for himself the cool breezes of the North Wind.[2] In the *Ebers Papyrus* it is stated that the breaths of life enter the body by the right

[1] Cf. A. H. Gardiner, *op. cit.*, p. 20.
[2] *Book of the Dead*, liv–lix.

ear and the breaths of death by the left,[1] and in another papyrus there is a prescription 'to banish death from the ear'.[2] Death in this conception is regarded, not as personified, but as a vague and invisible influence conveyed by air. It is noteworthy that the Egyptians, in whose religious ideas personification played so obtrusive a part, personified neither death nor life.[3] We will leave Egyptian ideas concerning death at this point, and return to them later.

The accidents that cause death (by whatever name it may be called) and however it may be understood, are nevertheless always menacingly at hand, and the interruption in the daily routine of active life that follows in their train has ever to be foreseen and guarded against. Hence arose the age-long quest of mankind for the Elixir of Life. In this striving after the preservation of youthful vigour man has made an endless series of compromises with fate to prolong his active existence by means of magic, by the use of amulets and of substances credited with life-giving power, and as a later development of these concepts, by medicine. Man has ever sought to repair by art the damage done to him by nature.

Violent death usually involves loss of blood, and hence it is probable that even as early as Aurignacian times, blood came to be regarded as the vital fluid which was essential to active existence. This belief will explain why blood plays such an important part

[1] *Papyrus Ebers*, 100, 2–4. See below, Chapter vi, p. 93.
[2] *Berlin Medical Papyrus*, 6, 11.
[3] For Egyptian personification see A. H. Gardiner, *Hastings' Encyclopædia of Religion and Ethics*, Vol. ix (Edinburgh 1916), pp. 787–792.

in the rites of primitive peoples, and why red objects
have ever been associated with blood and with death.
Primitive man buried his dead in red ochre, probably
with the object of supplying the vital stuff that was
lacking in the inert corpse and was essential to restore
it once more to activity. Instances of such burials
in red ochre are afforded by early human remains
buried in the Grotte des Enfants at Mentone, at
Predmost in Moravia, in the Dordogne Valley and
elsewhere in France. In 1823 a human skeleton,
stained red with ochre, was discovered in a cave at
Paviland, near Rhossilly in South Wales.[1] The same
motive has led these early races of man, as well as
many of their successors in various parts of the world,
to use red objects of various kinds to restore to the
body the vital substance lost at death. Red pebbles
and other red objects were buried with the dead,
red coffins, shrouds and other elements of the burial
equipment were inspired by the same desire as
prompted man of the Cro-Magnon race to bury his
dead in red ochre. In historic times the Egyptians
used an amulet of red carnelian or red jasper, that
typified the blood of the goddess Isis, which was
placed upon mummies in order to stimulate the
functions of the blood, or as a magical substitute
for the blood that was so conspicuously lacking in
the corpse.[2]

[1] D. A. Mackenzie, *Footprints of Early Man* (London
1927), pp. 66 *sq.*; D. Davidson, *Our Prehistoric Ancestors*
(London 1926), pp. 132 *sq.*; G. Elliot Smith, *The Evolution
of the Dragon* (Manchester 1919), pp. 145 *sq.*

[2] *Book of the Dead*, clxi; A. H. Gardiner, *The Tomb of
Amenemhēt* (London 1915), p. 112; G. Elliot Smith, *op. cit.*,
p. 150.

The belief in the life-giving attributes of blood is evident in many customs still practised in various parts of the world. Thus amongst the Central Australians in cases of severe illness human blood is swallowed as a medicine to impart renewed vitality to the patient : in such cases a man's blood is given to a woman and a woman's to a man.[1] Amongst the Tasmanian natives it was formerly the custom to administer human blood as a drink to a sick man.[2] Again, there exists the belief that a woman can cure her sick husband by rubbing his body with an ointment made of a mixture of fat and red ochre, the red ochre here, as elsewhere, being a substitute for blood.[3] A paste of fat and red clay is rubbed on their bodies by Kaffir women to strengthen them after childbirth,[4] and the Incas of Peru used to rub a paste of blood over their bodies as a protection against disease and weakness.[5] The blood drawn during the rite of circumcision and the menstrual blood of women is credited with special powers of life-giving because it originated in the life-giving organs. According to an Egyptian myth, the sun-god Rē mutilated himself, and the gods Hu and Sia sprang into existence from

[1] W. B. Spencer and F. J. Gillen, *The Native Tribes of Central Australia* (London 1899), p. 464 ; *The Arunta* (London 1927), Vol. ii, pp. 482 ff.

[2] J. Bonwick, *Daily Life and Origin of the Tasmanians* (London 1870), p. 89.

[3] W. B. Spencer and F. J. Gillen, *loc. cit.*

[4] J. Maclean, *A Compendium of Kafir Laws and Customs* (Cape Town 1858), p. 94.

[5] Garcilasso de la Vega, *Royal Commentaries of the Yncas* (ed. Sir Clements Markham), Hakluyt Soc. (London 1869–1871), Vol. ii, p. 228.

the blood which fell from his virile member.[1]   This
is probably the motive that originally was responsible
for the invention of circumcision.

Amongst many peoples to-day sacred trees are
sprinkled with blood to confer fertility and protection
upon them,[2] and there are myths that ascribe the
origin of trees and plants to blood.   In the well-
known Egyptian tale called ' The Story of the Two
Brothers ', two great acacia trees miraculously sprang
from two drops of blood which fell from the neck of
the slaughtered bull who was the reincarnation of
Bata, the hero of the story.[3]   According to another
myth, blood fell from the nose of the god Geb : ' the
blood grew, and thus came into existence the cedar-
tree, and from its sap came cedar-resin '.[4]   Similarly
in classical literature the tradition is preserved that
roses and anemones sprang from the blood of Adonis,
violets from the blood of Attis, and the purple iris
from the blood of Hyacinth.[5]

Violent death, caused by visible and material
agency, such as the foeman's axe or the fangs of wild
beasts, is regarded by many peoples in quite a different

---

[1] *Book of the Dead*, xvii.   A parallel instance in classical
tradition is afforded by the legend that the Erinyes sprang
from the blood that fell from the mutilated member of Uranos.
Hesiod, *Theogony*, 154 ff.

[2] For many examples see J. G. Frazer, *The Golden Bough*,
3rd ed.; *The Magic Art* (London 1911), Vol. ii, ch. 9.

[3] *Papyrus d'Orbiney* (Brit. Mus. No. 10,183), 16, 10 ; A.
Erman, *The Literature of the Ancient Egyptians* [transl. by
A. M. Blackman] (London 1927), p. 159 ; G. Maspero, *Popular
Stories of Ancient Egypt* (London 1915), p. 18.

[4] *Salt Magical Papyrus* (Brit. Mus. No. 10,051), 2, 2–3.

[5] J. G. Frazer, *The Golden Bough* (3rd ed.), *Adonis, Attis,
Osiris*, Vol. i (London 1914), p. 313.

light from death resulting from disease. The primitive
mind in such cases refuses to see in death any connection with the sickness that preceded it, or in any
sense the natural consequence or termination of illness.
The belief is almost universal that sickness and death
are unnatural and abnormal, and that they are manifestations of mischief caused by malign influence,
human or divine. Sickness is the result of one such
act of malignity; and death, if it follows, results
from another and quite separate act, not necessarily
emanating from the same source. In Queensland, for
instance, it is believed that sickness is caused by
some supernatural power,[1] and in South Australia
that it is the work of an enemy.[2] Elsewhere we find
disease attributed to a god, or to the dead, and the
same ideas are expressed in a phrase that often occurs
in Egyptian magical and medical texts that contain
spells or prescriptions for ridding a patient of suffering
that is called ' the assaults of a god, the assaults of
a goddess, of a dead man or of a dead woman, of an
enemy male or female, of an adversary, male or
female '.[3]

The refusal to admit death from sickness or from
natural causes is very widespread. It is a common
belief in Africa, and it is found in Indonesia, Melanesia
and many other parts of the world. Thus the con-

[1] W. E. Roth, *loc. cit., supra.*

[2] S. Gason, *Journal of the Anthropological Institute*, Vol.
xxiv (London 1895), p. 170. For Melanesian ideas on sickness
and death see W. H. R. Rivers, *Medicine, Magic and Religion*
(London 1924), pp. 5 ff.

[3] *Papyrus Leiden*, I, 348, verso 4, 3; *Ebers Papyrus*, I, 15,
and often in the magical texts.

nection between sickness and death is widely denied,
and also death from any other cause than battle,
murder or the attacks of wild beasts.   Even the latter
are often thought to be merely the agents of the
sorcerer.   What we call natural death is nearly always
attributed to witchcraft, sorcery, or divine interference in human affairs.   Such are the prevailing
ideas among primitive peoples to-day, and, by analogy,
such was probably the belief of primitive man before
the advent of civilization.

But if sickness did not cause death, death was
believed to cause sickness.   It has just been noted
that an Egyptian phrase voices the idea that sickness
and disease can be caused by ' the assaults of a dead
man or of a dead woman '.   A similar belief in the
danger of the dead to the living is found in many
parts of the world.   In Cambodia, for instance, the
dead are carried from their houses feet foremost ;
this is done in order that the dead man may not see
the house, in which event sickness would visit the
survivors.[1]   The Shilluks of the White Nile believe
that sickness is caused by the influence of their dead
kings, and they accordingly make sacrifices in order
to propitiate their royal tormentors.[2]   The Zulus
take medicine after a death in their kraal in order to
protect themselves from sickness.[3]   For the same
reason in other places houses in which a corpse lies

[1] E. Aymonier, *Cochinchine Française* (Saigon 1883), Vol.
vi, p. 202.

[2] J. G. Frazer, *The Golden Bough*, 3rd ed.; *The Dying God*
(London 1911), pp. 25 *sq.*

[3] D. Leslie, *Among the Zulus and Amatongas*, 2nd ed.
(Edinburgh 1875), p. 197.

are forsaken, or fires are lighted round them in order to keep out evil spirits which are attracted by the dead and would bring sickness upon the living. These and similar customs imply a belief in something very like contagion from the dead, and to protect himself against such risks the ingenuity of man has devised many measures. Thus the Navajos, when burying their dead, smear their bodies with tar in order to insulate themselves from evil influences, and any person who has touched or carried a corpse, removes all his clothes and bathes his body before mixing again with the living.[1] This contagion is a spiritual and not a physical one ; there is, of course, no idea of physical morbid infection by touching a dead body that had died of disease. The real fear is that the spirits residing in the corpse could transfer themselves or their influence to the living by mere contact. This belief underlies a host of customs and superstitions connected with the dead, many of which still persist even amongst civilized nations, and persons whose duties bring them into direct contact with dead bodies are always feared and avoided. It is thus that embalmers and other persons connected with mummifying the dead tend to become segregated into a separate caste. In Egypt, Diodorus Siculus tells us that the office of Embalmer was hereditary,[2] and this statement is borne out by other evidence in the Ptolemaic period.[3] In earlier times, the embalmers

---

[1] H. C. Yarrow, *Annual Report of the Bureau of American Ethnology* (Washington 1881), Vol. i, p. 123.

[2] Diodorus Siculus, *Bibliotheca Historica*, i, 91.

[3] E. Revillout, *Zeitschrift für ägyptische Sprache* (Leipsic, 1879), Vol. xvii, pp. 83–92.

appear to have constituted a distinct class or guild.[1] In the Canary Islands, the embalmers were regarded as unclean and treated as outcasts, although they were paid for their services.[2] The disfavour in which such persons were held is clearly shown in the statement of Diodorus Siculus, that the man who made the flank-incision in the body of an Egyptian during the process of mummification, had to take to his heels as soon as his duty had been performed, pursued by all those who had witnessed the act, who pelted him with missiles and with curses.[3] An exact parallel can be quoted from the islands of Torres Straits, where the man whose duty it was to cut off the head of a corpse for the purpose of embalming it, was obliged to flee from the relatives of the deceased who shot a shower of arrows at him.[4] Similarly in Tahiti, the embalmers were carefully avoided and were not even allowed to feed themselves : for if they handled food, all other food was liable to be affected with the taint of death, on the principle of sympathetic magic, by the contagion of the corpse the embalmers had touched.[5] Many other instances of penalties and taboos placed upon those who had come into contact with the dead have been collected by Sir James

[1] A. M. Blackman, art. 'Priest, Priesthood (Egyptian)' in *Hastings' Encyclopædia of Religion and Ethics*, Vol. x (Edinburgh 1916), p. 301.

[2] W. R. Dawson, *Proceedings of the Royal Society of Medicine*, Vol. xx (London 1926), p. 837.

[3] Diodorus Siculus, *loc. cit.*

[4] *Report of the Cambridge Anthropological Expedition to Torres Straits*, Vol. v (Cambridge 1904), pp. 249 *sq.*

[5] W. Ellis, *Polynesian Researches* (London 1859), Vol. iv, p. 388.

Frazer.[1] The hatred or avoidance of those who ceremonially touched or mutilated the dead was not originally due to respect or reverence for the dead, but to the fear that the influence of the corpse might harm the living.

Such notions as have been described above gave rise to the necessity of exercising ingenuity in order to foil, or to appease, the powers that inflicted illness and death and to avenge their victims. The need also asserted itself of securing continuity of existence in spite of all the manifold attempts, human and divine, to bring about its extinction. Around this determination has grown the vast edifice of diverse customs and beliefs, of religions and philosophies, of ceremonies and rituals, many of which betray a common origin. It was out of this determination to thwart hostile powers that the rôles of the magician, of the doctor, and to a large extent also of the priest, came into being. The magician with his spells, the doctor with his medicines and the priest with his prayers and ritual, have laboured for countless centuries to protect and prolong life, to confer vitality and to impede the powers that threaten existence. In the earliest times amulets were worn by the living and buried with the dead to accomplish these ends. Shells, perhaps the earliest symbols of life, played an obtrusive part in this system of protective magic : they were worn by the living to facilitate birth and were bestowed upon the dead to ensure rebirth.

Beliefs in immortality and a future life arose out of the attempts of early man to prolong his earthly

---

[1] *The Golden Bough*, ed. 3; *Taboo and the Perils of the Soul* (London 1911), pp. 138 *sq.*

existence, and these endeavours took definite shape in Egypt where the art was learned, not only of preventing the dissolution of the body, but of preserving the form and personal identity of the dead. The circumstances that gave rise to the art of mummification five thousand years ago, we shall consider in the next chapter. This strange and distinctive custom has played an enormous part not only in religious history, but in shaping the destinies of mankind. Ethnologists have as yet scarcely begun to recognize how great this influence has been.

CHAPTER II

PROLONGING LIFE AND AVERTING
EXTINCTION

IN Egypt during the long period of advancing civilization that preceded the First Dynasty (c. 3400 B.C.) it was the custom to bury the dead by inhumation in the sands of the desert. Cultivable land was too valuable for such a purpose, and indeed, had it been the custom to bury the dead in the moist, loamy soil adjoining the river, we should have no knowledge of the early civilization of the Nile Valley, for all its records must inevitably have decayed. By burying their dead in the hot, dry, desert sands, the predynastic Egyptians confided to nature not only the preservation of their actual bodies, but all the equipment with which they provided them and which enables us to reconstruct the culture of that distant age. The dead were buried in a flexed position, sometimes loosely wrapped in skins or mats and sometimes without such coverings in shallow graves, and completely covered with sand. The result of this method of burial has been, wherever circumstances were favourable, the entire preservation of the body by desiccation. Thanks to the dry climate and the preservative effect of direct contact with the sand, so perfectly has nature preserved the remains of these

17

early dwellers in the Nile Valley, that it is possible to examine anatomically the soft and perishable parts of the body and even to ascertain the nature of the food they ate by scrutinizing the contents of the alimentary canal.

From the stomachs and intestines of these prehistoric people it has been possible to recover large quantities of food-materials—the last meals eaten before death. The scientific examination of these specimens has rendered it possible to discover not only the nature of predynastic Egyptian diet, but also some knowledge of the methods employed to prepare food for consumption. Husks of barley were identified in almost every specimen, and in a number of cases those of millet were also found. The finding of millet is of great interest, because its use in Egypt has been denied, and the species found is not now cultivated except in the East Indies. Root-tubers of *Cyperus esculentus* were found, and also the remains of other plants, together with abundant traces of fish, for the predynastic Egyptians made and used metal fish-hooks. These points are worthy of mention, because they show how much the natural conditions of Egypt have aided modern research in the investigation of early civilization ; nowhere else in the world have circumstances been so favourable.[1]

There are good reasons for believing that this wonderful phenomenon of natural preservation in Egypt suggested the earliest attempts to preserve the body by artificial means—in other words, to make mummies—a custom that had reached a high stage

[1] G. Elliot Smith, *The Ancient Egyptians*, 2nd ed. (London 1923), pp. 48 *sq*.

of development by the time the Pyramids were built. The natural preservation of the dead was probably first made known to the Egyptians by the ravages of tomb-robbers and of jackals, whose depredations exposed the hapless bodies to view. The discovery that the corpses of the dead did not suffer corruption probably originated, and undoubtedly strengthened, the belief in the physical survival of the dead, a belief that underlies the practice of mummification throughout the historic period. Such a belief prompted the ampler provision of food, utensils and a host of other objects necessary to physical life that were buried with the dead. As the number of objects placed in the grave increased, the grave itself had to be made more spacious to accommodate these larger supplies. The grave was roofed over with boughs, beams or slabs of stone, or a chamber was cut in solid rock, or lined with mud-bricks, and the burial of the dead in these roomier graves or in constructed tombs defeated the very object that had inspired the more lavish burial equipment. For the body was no longer embedded in dry, desiccating sand, but lay in a space filled with air, which promoted decomposition: the body accordingly decayed and the dead man did not survive to enjoy the use of the objects with which he was surrounded. Thus arose the attempt to achieve by art the preservation of the body which unaided nature could no longer accomplish in the larger tombs.[1]

[1] G. Elliot Smith, *The Evolution of the Dragon* (Manchester 1919), p. 15 ; *Egyptian Mummies* (London 1924), pp. 23 *sq.* ; W. R. Dawson, art. 'Mummy', *Encyclopædia Britannica*, 14th ed.

3

It is probable that attempts at mummification were being made, at least in the case of the bodies of royal personages, as early as the First Dynasty (*c.* 3400 B.C.). The nature of the royal tombs explored by Flinders Petrie suggests great elaboration in the burial customs of this remote period.[1] In one of these tombs a human arm torn from a body was found. Upon this arm, which was wrapped in linen bandages, bracelets of First Dynasty date were found. This interesting specimen was sent to the Cairo Museum, but it has unfortunately disappeared, so that it is not possible to make an examination of it for the purpose of eliciting evidence as to the method of preservation employed. Petrie states: ' The flesh is dried upon the bones and wrapped in a thick mass of the finest linen, 120 threads by 160 threads to the inch, saturated with oils or resins.'[2] There is no trace of flesh upon the bones shown in the published photograph,[3] but the fact that the limb was wrapped in linen, an essential feature of mummification, is of itself presumptive evidence that artificial embalming had been attempted.

The earliest definite evidence of an attempt of mummification is afforded by a body of the Second Dynasty discovered at Sakkara in 1911 by J. E. Quibell. The body was that of a woman about 35 years of age and was lying in a flexed position on

[1] See his memoirs published by the Egypt Exploration Society, *Royal Tombs of the Earliest Dynasties* (2 vols. London 1900–1) and *Abydos* (3 vols. London 1902–4).

[2] *Cairo Scientific Journal*, Vol. ii (Cairo 1908), p. 204.

[3] Petrie, *Royal Tombs of the Earliest Dynasties*, Part ii (London 1901), Pl. i.

the left side in a wooden coffin. The body was completely enwrapped in a complex series of bandages—more than sixteen layers still intact, and probably at least as many more destroyed : ten layers of fine linen bandage, then six layers of somewhat coarser cloth, and next to the body a mass of much corroded very irregularly woven cloth, much coarser than the outer layers. Each limb was separately wrapped. In the wide interval between the bandages and the bones, there was a large mass of extremely corroded linen, whereas the intermediate and superficial layers were quite well preserved and free from corrosion, except along a line where the cloth was corroded to represent the *rima pudendi*—a fact of great interest when it is recalled that in male mummies of the Pyramid Age it was the custom to fashion an artificial phallus. The corrosion of the innermost layers of wrappings suggest that some material, probably crude natron, had been applied to the surface of the body in order to preserve it.[1] Similarly treated bodies belonging to the Third and Fourth Dynasties were found by Garstang at Beni Hasan, but he did not recognize that any attempt at mummification had been made.[2]

In 1891, a remarkable mummy was discovered at Meidûm by Petrie, who presented it to the Museum of the Royal College of Surgeons in London. The body had been wrapped in large quantities of linen

[1] G. Elliot Smith, *Report, British Association, Dundee,* 1912 (London 1913), p. 612 ; *Journal of Egyptian Archæology,* Vol. i (London 1914), p. 192, Pl. xxxi.

[2] J. Garstang, *Burial Customs of Ancient Egypt* (London 1907), pp. 29–30, fig. 18.

bandage of various textures, and the outermost
layers were saturated with resin. The embalmers
had carefully moulded the form of the body, paying
special attention to the details of the head, the
features being indicated by means of paint. This
resinous linen set to form a carapace of stony hard-
ness, and upon it the genital organs are modelled
with minute precision. The viscera had been removed
through an incision in the left flank, and the remains
of them, made up into packets, were discovered in
the tomb. One of these packets has since been
identified as the liver.[1] The body is in the fully
extended position which from this period onwards
supersedes the contracted attitude of the earlier
burials, and is in a wonderful state of preservation.
It must probably be assigned to the Fifth Dynasty.[2]
Remains of another mummy of this period were
found in the same locality twenty years later.[3] A
similarly prepared mummy of the Old Kingdom
(probably Sixth Dynasty) was found by Reisner at
Gizeh,[4] and another of the Fifth Dynasty by Petrie
at Deshasheh.[5]

During the Middle Kingdom the art of embalming

[1] M. A. Ruffer, *Studies in the Palæopathology of Egypt*
(Chicago 1921), p. 12.

[2] W. M. F. Petrie, *Meydum* (London 1892), p. 18; G. Elliot
Smith, *Journal of Egyptian Archæology*, Vol. i (London 1914),
p. 192, and Pl. xxxi, fig. 2; *The Evolution of the Dragon*
(Manchester 1919), p. 16, and fig. 2.

[3] W. M. F. Petrie, *Meydum and Memphis III* (London
1910), pp. 4, 15, 16 and Pl. xi.

[4] G. A. Reisner, *Museum of Fine Arts Bulletin* (Boston,
U.S.A., 1913), Vol. xi, No. 66, p. 58.

[5] W. M. F. Petrie, *Deshasheh* (London 1898), p. 15.

deteriorated somewhat. Owing to the less lavish
use of resin, and probably also to imperfect desiccation, most of the mummies of this period are very
fragile and ill-preserved. A careful examination of
them, however, shows that the custom of macerating
the body in a salt-bath had been introduced, but no
attempt had as yet been made to remove the
brain.[1]

Early in the New Kingdom (Eighteenth–Twentieth
Dynasties) numerous improvements in method were
introduced. The brain was removed by forcing a
passage into the skull, a more effective method of
desiccation was employed, and greater skill had been
acquired in the preparation and application of the
resinous preservative material with which the body
was treated. Many mummies of this period have
been discovered, but our principal source of information is the great series of royal mummies that was
discovered in 1881 and 1898, and which are now in
the Cairo Museum. Although these bodies had all
been mutilated by tomb-robbers, many of them are
splendid examples of the embalmer's art.[2] To this
series of royal mummies, subsequent discoveries have

[1] For details of mummies of the Middle Kingdom, see
G. Elliot Smith and W. R. Dawson, *Egyptian Mummies* (London
1924), pp. 78–86.
[2] The discovery of the first batch of royal mummies is
dealt with at length by G. Maspero, *Les Momies Royales de
Deir-el-Bahari*, Paris 1889, and the second by V. Loret,
Bulletin de l'Institut Egyptien, 3rd ser. No. 9 (Cairo 1899),
pp. 91–112. The mummies were re-examined and minutely
described by G. Elliot Smith, *The Royal Mummies* (Cairo
1912).

added the Mummies of Yuaa and Thuiu,[1] of Prince
Maherpra[2] and of the Pharaoh Tutankhamen.[3]

An account of the process of making a mummy
based principally upon the examination of mummies
of the New Kingdom will be given in the next chapter,
so for the moment it is unnecessary to enter into any
details of the technique of the period, but we will
proceed to consider the methods employed in the
Twenty-first and Twenty-second Dynasties when the
art reached its highest pitch of perfection. For our
knowledge of the details of this period, we are indebted
to Professor G. Elliot Smith, who first described the
remarkable technique from an examination of forty-
four specimens.[4]

During the reign of the priest-king Hrihor, the
first sovereign of the Twenty-first Dynasty, and of
his immediate successors great activity was displayed
in restoring the plundered remains of the kings of
the three preceding dynasties. The robbers in their
search for treasure had hacked away the bandages
and damaged the bodies, and the pious restorers had

[1] G. Elliot Smith in J. E. Quibell, *Tomb of Yuaa and Thuiu*
(Cairo 1908), pp. 68–73.

[2] G. Daressy, *Fouilles de la Vallée des Rois*, Iere partie
(Cairo 1901) ; W. R. Dawson, *Proceedings of the Royal Society
of Medicine*, Vol. xx (London 1927), pp. 842 *sq.*

[3] D. E. Derry in Howard Carter, *The Tomb of Tutankhamen*,
Vol. ii (London 1927), pp. 143 *sq.*

[4] G. Elliot Smith, ' Contributions to the Study of Mummification ', *Mémoires presentés à l'Institut Egyptien*, Vol. v
(Cairo 1906), pp. 1–53 and Pls. i–xix. This memoir, and his
monograph, *The Royal Mummies* (Cairo 1912), are the founda-
tions of all our scientific knowledge of the technique and
significance of mummification.

set about rebandaging these battered remains. In the course of doing so, they must have been impressed by the failure of the embalmer's art to preserve the life-like appearance of their predecessors, and this was probably the motive that led to a determined attempt to improve the craft of mummification. It is at least apparent that immediately after the striking object lesson afforded by the handling of the royal mummies of the Eighteenth to Twentieth Dynasties, the embalmers of the Twenty-first Dynasty set to work to devise some means of restoring to the mummy the fulness of limb and features that it had possessed during life but had lost during the process of embalming.

With this object in view they devised an elaborate method of introducing packing material under the skin in order to plump out the body which had shrunken during the immersion in the salt-bath. The embalmers separated the skin from the under-lying muscular tissue, and tunnelled a number of channels with some pointed instrument. Into these channels mud, sand or other material was forced and distributed over the contours of the body by massage. This packing was introduced partly by way of the embalming-wound, and partly through a schematic series of incisions made for the purpose in various parts of the body. Great skill was acquired in this highly difficult process, and packing material was inserted in all parts of the body and limbs, with the result that the finished mummy revealed the round-ness and fulness of contour of a living body, in sharp contrast with the wrinkled and deflated appearance of mummies of earlier periods. In order to make the body more life-like, it was painted all over with red

ochre (yellow ochre being used for women), the cheeks
and lips were rouged, and artificial eyes were inserted
under the eyelids. In order to make the body, not
only life-like, but whole and complete, the internal
organs were wrapped in linen parcels and returned to
the body-cavity, the custom of placing them in
Canopic jars being discontinued. All the details of
this remarkable method of embalming have been
described in the memoir referred to, and further
examples of bodies preserved in this way were found
amongst the royal mummies, and others have been
discovered in more recent years.

After the Twenty-second Dynasty, the art of
mummification declined. In the Twenty-fifth and
Twenty-sixth dynasties, the embalmers still produced
well-preserved mummies, but they had abandoned the
elaborate methods of their predecessors.[1] The technique of the mummies of the Twenty-third and
Twenty-fourth Dynasties is a compromise between
the methods in vogue before and after that period.[2]
During the last dynasties and throughout the Ptolemaic
and Roman periods, although well-made mummies
are occasionally found, the art of embalming steadily
deteriorated. Less care was devoted to the body,
and more to the external wrappings, so as to give the
mummy a presentable exterior. The body was sometimes eviscerated in the usual way, but more often
it was merely covered with molten resin that often
charred or destroyed the tissues and made a mere

[1] W. R. Dawson, *Journal of Egyptian Archæology*, Vol.
xiii (London 1927), pp. 157-158.
[2] W. R. Dawson, *Proceedings of the Society of Antiquaries
of Scotland*, Vol. lxi (Edinburgh 1928), pp. 294-296.

cast, roughly in the form of the body. After the advent of Christianity, mummification was still practised, but in a different manner. The old methods of evisceration and treatment with resin were given up, and the bodies were merely packed in large quantities of common salt, but are usually very well preserved.[1]

Such in outline is the history of mummification in Egypt over a period of more than thirty centuries. The practice played a very important part in the great religious and philosophical edifice which grew up around it, and which has persisted throughout the ages in varying forms since it first seemed to offer to men the means of averting extinction and of obtaining continuity of existence. Throughout its long career, the practice of mummification had two definite objects in view : first, the preservation of the body from decay, and secondly, the perpetuation of the personal identity of the deceased. It has already been noted that during the Pyramid Age, the features of the mummy were painted on the outer wrappings, and in some cases, a thin layer of plaster was applied to the head and the features painted upon it.[2] In the Eleventh Dynasty the face and wig were modelled in a kind of pasteboard known as cartonage, and this head-piece was placed over the head of the mummy.

[1] For details of mummification in the later periods, see G. Elliot Smith and F. Wood-Jones, *Report on the Human Remains* (Archæological Survey of Nubia, Report for 1907–8, Vol. ii, Cairo 1910), and the summary in G. Elliot Smith and W. R. Dawson, *Egyptian Mummies* (London 1924), pp. 121–132.

[2] H. Junker, *Journal of Egyptian Archæology*, Vol. i (London 1914), p. 252.

The use of cartonage masks lasted until Ptolemaic times, but out of it was early evolved the anthropoid coffin, on which the features, dress and ornaments of the mummy were elaborately detailed. In Roman times, painted portrait-panels were used.[1] All these devices had one object—the preservation of the dead man's personal identity by the portrayal of his features which were hidden beneath the bandages. That the idea underlying mummification was physical survival is further indicated by the magical ceremonies to which the finished mummy was subjected. These ceremonies, which are usually known as 'Opening the Mouth', had for their object the reanimation of the mummy by restoring to it the faculties of which death and embalming had temporarily deprived it. By means of magical instruments and the recitation of formulæ, the eyes, mouth and ears of the dead man were opened in order that he might once more see, speak, eat and hear. The use of his limbs was restored to him that he might move and walk and exercise all the bodily functions of a living man.[2] Amulets were placed upon the mummy to stimulate the functions of the heart, the spine and the blood,[3] and incense and libations were ceremonially employed to restore to the desiccated mummy the warmth and

[1] For a fine series of coloured reproductions of these panels, see W. M. F. Petrie, *The Hawara Portfolio* (London 1913).

[2] For the ceremonies of 'Opening the Mouth', see E. Schiaparelli, *Il Libro dei Funerali*, 3 vols. (Rome 1882–1890); E. A. W. Budge, *The Book of Opening the Mouth*, 2 vols. (London 1909); G. Maspero, *Etudes de Mythologie*, Vol. i (Paris 1893), pp. 283–324; A. H. Gardiner, *The Tomb of Amenemhēt* (London 1915), pp. 57 *sq.*

[3] A. H. Gardiner, *op. cit.*, p. 112.

moisture of a living body.[1] The funerary banquet that followed was envisaged, not as spiritual food for the soul, but as material and physical sustenance to be consumed by the mummy with its restored faculties.[2] The elaborate equipment of the tomb with objects of use or ornament, of which the tomb of Tutankhamen has provided such a striking instance, likewise affirms the notion of physical survival, and the fact that in some tombs privies were provided for the use of the dead, clearly demonstrates how literally this physical existence after death was envisaged.[3]

As will be seen in the sequel, many of the drugs used by the Egyptians in medicine, even when appropriate and rational, were originally introduced into the pharmacopœia for purely magical reasons. In the same way natron, salt and resin, all of which are excellent preservatives, were probably first employed in mummification because these substances were credited with life-giving, or life-preserving, properties. Natron was used in the daily ceremonies connected with the rebirth of the sun-god,[4] the life-giving power

[1] A. M. Blackman, *Zeitschrift für ägyptische Sprache*, Vol. 50 (Leipsic 1912), pp. 69 *sq.*; G. Elliot Smith, *The Evolution of the Dragon* (Manchester 1919), pp. 23 *sq.*

[2] E. A. W. Budge, *The Liturgy of Funerary Offerings* (London 1909), p. ix, is wrong when he states that the object of the ceremonies was to change the offerings into spiritual food for the soul.

[3] J. E. Quibell, *Report, British Association*, 1914 meeting (London 1915), p. 215.

[4] A. M. Blackman, *Journal of Egyptian Archæology*, Vol. v (London 1918), pp. 117 *sq.* and 148 *sq.*; art. 'Purification (Egyptian)' in *Hastings' Encyclopædia of Religion and Ethics*, Vol. x (Edinburgh 1916).

of salt was a tradition that survived until classical times,[1] and resin was believed to be the blood or some other bodily emanation of the god Osiris.[2] When therefore the necessity for artificial preservation of the dead first became apparent, it was natural that the attempt to confer or prolong life, should have taken the form of applying to the corpse substances that were believed to possess divine or magical potency to that end.

The custom of mummification has had a profound influence on the growth of medical science, although it was a religious observance and was carried out, not by medical men but by priests. Further reference to this point will be made when dealing with Egyptian notions of anatomy and physiology. Before passing on to the study of Egyptian medicine, some description will be given of the actual manipulative processes to which the embalmers subjected the dead body : this will make clearer the extent to which the custom of embalming influenced medical knowledge.

[1] Cf. Plutarch, *Symposiacs*, v, 10.
[2] Maspero, *Etude sur quelques papyrus du Louvre* (Paris 1875), p. 57.

CHAPTER III

MAKING A MUMMY [1]

IN the preceding chapter the history of the custom of mummification was sketched in outline. It is now necessary to examine in greater detail the actual manipulations of the embalmer, and to show how these practices influenced the growth of the science of anatomy. Much has already been written on the subject of mummification, but a prolonged study of the literature has convinced me that most of the accounts we possess of the technique of Egyptian embalming abound in errors and omissions. In the course of this enquiry I have read and annotated scores of accounts by various writers between the time of Herodotus and the present day,[2] but many of them describe processes that it would be impossible to put into operation, and the examination of a large series of actual mummies of various periods has

---

[1] This chapter is based, with some modifications, upon an article that I contributed to the *Journal of Egyptian Archæology*, Vol. xiii (1927), pp. 40–49.

[2] I have prepared a critical bibliography of works on Egyptian mummification, with epitomes and notes, that will shortly be published by the Institut d'Egypte, and passages in the works of classical writers relating to the subject I have collected and published in *Ægyptus*, Vol. ix (Milan 1928), pp. 106–112.

revealed to me many details that the writers do not take into account at all. With the exception of the works of Prof. Elliot Smith, to whom we are indebted for almost all our scientific knowledge of mummification and its significance, and of a few others, the majority of accounts of mummification even by modern writers are of little value. I shall therefore attempt to describe in outline all the manipulations to which the body of an Egyptian was subjected between the day of his death and that of his funeral. In spite of the foregoing strictures on the accounts of the older writers, I hasten to say that there are certain notable exceptions. The observations of Rouyer, Granville and Pettigrew (to name but three), considering their materials and the state of knowledge of Egyptian archæology which existed in their day, are contributions of the highest value, and embody much original research.

This account is based mainly upon the technique of the New Kingdom, and I have generalized as far as possible in describing procedure which varied in certain details from time to time, and almost from reign to reign. Full particulars of these details will be found in Elliot Smith's descriptions of the royal mummies at Cairo and in various other monographs he has written. He has, in the main, described the mummies themselves, that is to say the *results* of the various manipulations of the embalmers : I have endeavoured to reconstruct in consecutive order the various processes employed to obtain those results. I have chosen the above specified period because we have insufficient material to deal at all fully with the earlier periods, and because in the Twenty-first

Dynasty, as already indicated, a new and elaborate method was introduced, a description of the details of which would not only require too much space but is moreover needless, since Elliot Smith, who first discovered this peculiar technique, has already worked the subject out in the fullest possible manner.[1] I shall, however, note the principal variations in method revealed by the earlier and later mummies respectively in their appropriate places.

The whole process of mummification, it is almost superfluous to say, was one of profound religious significance, and the embalmers and their assistants impersonated the gods who figured in the mythological embalming of Osiris. The embalmer's chamber was consequently not a mere workshop, but in a sense a kind of shrine in which certain prescribed rites were performed. From the general statements made in various Egyptological books we have become accustomed to think of the embalmer's workshop as a permanent establishment, like a mortuary or an anatomical theatre, to which bodies were taken for treatment. This notion has arisen from the use of such expressions as 'the embalmer's laboratory', 'the embalmer's studio' and the like. There is no evidence, however, that any such permanent establishment existed, but there is evidence which seems to leave no doubt that the workshop was a temporary structure or tent, erected for each person as occasion arose, and that, having fulfilled its purpose, it was dismantled. Certain texts speak specifically of '*thy*

[1] *Contribution to the Study of Mummification in Egypt.* (Mémoires présentés à l'Institut Égyptien, tome v, fasc. 1, Cairo 1906.)

place of embalming ', or ' *his* place of embalming ',
which again implies that each person had his own.[1]
The usual Egyptian word for the embalming place is
w'bt, ' pure place ', or *w'bt nt pr nfr*, ' pure place of
the Good House '.　It was probably erected near the
tomb of the deceased, but in any case it was in the
necropolis, far removed from the habitations of the
living, for on the death of a person his body was conveyed to the embalmer's shed, probably with appropriate ceremony.　In the tomb of Pepionkh at Mêr
there is a scene labelled ' escorting to the workshop
of the embalmer '.[2]　The word *w'bt* occurs in texts
of all periods from the Old Kingdom to Roman
times.

Another phrase of frequent occurrence is *syh ntr*,
' tent of the god ', or ' god's booth '.　The temporary
nature of the embalmer's workshop is again indicated
by this word.

In the tent or kiosk of the embalmer the whole
process of mummification was carried out, and it
occupied a period of seventy days.[3]　The actual
manipulative processes could have been completed in
a much shorter time, but it must be remembered that
the whole ceremony was a religious one, and was
carried out in conformity with a definite ritual, one
or more priests being present during a great part of
the time reciting formulæ as each manipulation was

[1] A. H. Gardiner, *The Tomb of Amenemhēt*, p. 56.
[2] *Ibid.*, p. 45, n. 4.
[3] To the instances relating to the seventy-day period collected in Elliot Smith and Dawson, *Egyptian Mummies*
(London 1924), pp. 53 ff., must be added *Papyrus Rylands
IX*, p. 10, l. 10.

completed, and the period was consequently much protracted. We have references to this canon or ritual in the inscription of Anemher, where the expression 'according to that which comes in writing' follows each ceremony or process enumerated.[1] In addition to this we have the remains of the ritual which was used during the lengthy process of anointing and bandaging the mummy,[2] and finally, in various pictures in certain tombs at Thebes, to be mentioned later, an officiating priest armed with a papyrus-roll is seen superintending the manipulations of the embalmers.

On its arrival at the workshop, the body was first stripped, then laid upon a board or platform. One of these boards has actually been found: it is a wooden platform 7 feet 1 inch long, and 4 feet 2½ inches wide, and is provided with transverse battens, and was probably supported upon two blocks or trestles.[3] A wicker-work bier which had served the same purpose was discovered in similar circumstances two years later.[4] In the conventional representation of embalming a mummy, which is an extremely common decorative device on coffins, and is also represented in the vignette to Chapter 151 of the Book of the Dead, the mummy is shown lying upon a lion-headed bier attended by the embalmer who impersonated the

[1] Brugsch, *Thesaurus*, p. 893 ; Griffith, *High Priests of Memphis*, p. 29 ; Elliot Smith and Dawson, *op. cit.*, p. 54.

[2] The so-called 'Ritual of Embalming', published by G. Maspero, *Mémoire sur quelques papyrus du Louvre*, Paris 1875.

[3] H. E. Winlock, *Bulletin of the Metrop. Mus. New York*, Part ii, Dec. 1922, p. 34.

[4] H. E. Winlock, *op. cit.*, 1924, Part ii, 32.

4

god Anubis, and wears a jackal-headed mask.[1] Probably this ornate lion-couch was not really used until the process of actual embalming was nearly finished, and the mummy merely awaited the final ceremonies. The kings had three such couches, one with a cow's, the second with a lion's and the third with a hippopotamus' head, as we know from the pictures in the tomb of Seti I, the fragments found in the tomb of Haremhab, and the complete specimens in the tomb of Tutankhamen.[2] These luxurious biers were almost certainly not used until the ' dirty work ' of evisceration and anointing had been completed.

The first process to be performed was the extraction of the brain. I have elsewhere described this feat in detail,[3] and need make no further reference to it than to point out that a passage was forced with a chisel through the nostril (usually the left) and the ethmoid bone into the cranial-cavity. This was the normal procedure, but sometimes the operator missed the ethmoid, and broke through the sphenoid. Considerable force was used to effect this fracture, which often did much damage to the facial skeleton. A metal rod, hooked at the end, was then inserted, and the membranes and tissues of the brain were lacerated and reduced to fragments by this means. The broken brain was then removed piecemeal by means of another

[1] Anubis was *par excellence* the god of embalming. A frequent title of this god is ' Chief of the god's tent '. An actual mask in the shape of a jackal's head which was used by the embalmer has been found, and is figured in F. Lexa, *La magie dans l'Égypte antique* (Paris 1925), Pl. xxxiii.

[2] Elliot Smith, *Tutankhamen and the Discovery of his Tomb,* 109.

[3] *Proc. Roy. Soc. Medicine,* vii, xx, 1927, p. 844.

rod, the end of which was spirally twisted so as to form a kind of spatula.[1] In many cases every particle of brain has been so completely removed, that it is evident that the cranial-cavity had been irrigated with a corrosive fluid in order to wash it out. It often happens however that the operation was less carefully performed and fragments of the brain were left behind. There were other methods of removing the brain which did not involve a forced passage through the nose, and these I have described in the memoir referred to. For the moment the cranial-cavity received no further treatment. The mouth was washed out, and then stuffed with resin-soaked linen, and sometimes also the ears. The face was then thickly coated with resinous paste. The eyes, which were not ablated, collapsed into the orbits, and pads of linen were placed over them and the lids drawn over this packing material. In the Twenty-first and Twenty-second Dynasties artificial eyes of obsidian or some other suitable material were placed over the shrunken eyeballs, and the lids adjusted, but not closed.

The next process was the removal of the viscera. Herodotus tells us that an incision was made in the flank (Diodorus specifically says the *left* flank) through which the entrails were removed and washed. The examination of scores of mummies of all periods from the Fourth Dynasty onwards proves the truth of these assertions, for the embalming-wound is found almost always on the left side. I know of only two

[1] For the implements used in mummification, see K. Sudhoff, *Ägyptische Mumienmacher-Instrumente*, in *Archiv für Gesch. der Medizin*, v (1912), pp. 161–171 and 2 plates.

recorded cases in which the right flank has been incised.[1] The embalmer inserted his hand through the incision, and with a knife severed all the organs from their connections. The abdominal viscera were first removed, then an incision was made in the diaphragm, and through this opening and the original flank-incision, the operator inserted his arm and removed the thoracic viscera, except the heart, which was always carefully left *in situ* attached to its great vessels. Diodorus tells us that the kidneys also were left in the body, and in some instances they have actually been so found, but the rule was not invariable as it was in the case of the heart. Except when through clumsy or careless manipulation the heart was accidentally severed (in which case it was left either lying loose in the thorax or else attached by a ligament) it is always to be found in its place. This fact has great significance when considered in relation to certain Egyptian texts, but the subject is one into which we cannot enter now. Elliot Smith demonstrated this fact years ago, but still the time-honoured fallacy is repeated, that the heart was taken from the body and placed with the other viscera in a Canopic jar.[2]

The exact situation of the embalming-wound varied from time to time and its position, taken in conjunc-

[1] F. Wood-Jones, *Arch. Surv. Nubia*, Report for 1907–8, ii [*Report on the Human Remains*] (Cairo 1910), p. 206 ; E. A. W. Budge, *Prefatory Remarks on Egyptian Mummies . . . The Mummy of Bak-ran* (London 1890), p. 25.

[2] For the treatment of the heart, see especially G. Elliot Smith, *Contribution*, etc. (*op. cit.*, *supra*), pp. 17 and 28, and *Heart and Reins* in the *Journ. Manchester Oriental Soc.*, Vol. i (1911), pp. 45 ff.

tion with various other details of technique, is a valuable indication of date. In the early part of the Eighteenth Dynasty, the embalming-wound was a vertical incision, extending upward from near the anterior superior spine of the ilium towards the ribs. Later in the same dynasty, in the time of Tuthmosis III, a change was made, and the incision was cut downwards from the same point, taking an oblique course parallel to Poupart's ligament. Later on the vertical position was resumed.[1] Herodotus states that the body-cavity was next washed and filled with myrrh and other preservative agents, then sewn up, and soaked in natron for seventy days. His account is here at fault in several particulars. In the first place, it would have been wasted labour and entirely ineffectual to have filled the cavity with spices *before* its long immersion : in the second place, the custom of sewing up the wound, whilst not unknown, is so extremely rare as to be the exception and not the rule : in the third place, seventy days was the period occupied by the entire process of mummification, not merely the salting-process alone, which we know from various Egyptian texts to have occupied only part of that time. The actual procedure after removal of the viscera was merely to wash out the body-cavity, and then to immerse the corpse in the salt-bath. During this long immersion the epidermis peeled off, taking with it all the body-hair, and it was for this reason also that special care was taken to secure the nails so that they should not come away with the macerated skin and be lost. To accomplish this end, the embalmers cut the skin round the base

[1] G. Elliot Smith, *The Royal Mummies*, pp. 33-4.

of the nail of each finger and toe, so as to form a natural thimble of skin. Around each such thimble they wound a thread or a twist of wire to hold the nail in its place.[1] In the case of kings and wealthy persons, the thimbles of skin with their nails were kept in position by means of metal stalls. The mummy of Tut'ankhamūn had a set of gold stalls in position. It is specially to be noted that the head was not immersed, for it always retains the epidermis and the hair (unless the scalp had been previously shaved) and does not present the same appearance of emaciation as the rest of the body.

It has generally been assumed that the salt-bath was a long tank in which the body lay horizontally: but a little reflexion will show that if this were the case, it would be impossible to prevent the immersion of the head. I believe that the salt-bath was a large jar, in which the body was placed in a sharply flexed position, the liquid being poured in to the level of the neck, and maintained at that level after loss by absorption and evaporation. The head, while thus exposed, was preserved from disintegration by a thick coating of resinous paste. In order to accommodate the corpse to the confined space of the jar, it would have been necessary to double it into the smallest possible compass. This method of immersing the body (excluding the head) was suggested to my mind by the extremely contracted position in which Peruvian and Australian mummies are found. It will be observed that these mummies are in a position

[1] The nails were affixed in exactly the same manner by the Guanches of the Canary Islands. See my paper, *Proc. Roy. Soc. Med.*, Vol. xx (1927), p. 839.

of extreme contraction and are not in the attitude assumed by the normal posture of a sitting man. The legs are bent sharply on themselves and compressed tightly against the body, and in some Australian mummies the knees are trussed up into so unnatural a position that they are actually forced behind the shoulders : in other examples the limbs are bound tightly to the body, the whole being made into a compact bundle. Peruvian mummies are similarly compressed.[1] The intention in these cases is evidently to pack the body into the smallest possible compass. Dr. Blackman, who has made a special study of the significance of lustrations amongst the Egyptians, has collected a series of representations from tombs of the Middle and New Kingdoms, which depict in a highly conventionalized manner the washing of the corpse after it is taken out of the salt-bath, and before its final anointing and bandaging. In some of these scenes the corpse is represented in a sitting posture above a large jar, whilst the embalmer and a priest pour a stream of lustration-water over it. The whole scene is ceremonial in character, and is borrowed, as Dr. Blackman has emphasized, from the daily temple ritual of the king, and adapted to the ritual of embalming.[2] The washing of the corpse after its immersion in the salt-bath, however much it may have been formalized and invested with religious significance,

[1] See the illustrations in my paper 'Mummification in Australia and in America', *Journal of the Royal Anthropological Inst.*, Vol. lviii (1928), pp. 115–138, Pls. 8–13, and in *Man*, 1928, No. 53, with Pl. E.

[2] *Recueil de Travaux*, Vol. 39, 1921, pp. 47–78, especially pp. 53–55 ; see also his article 'Washing the Dead', *Journal of Egyptian Archæology*, Vol. v (1918), pp. 117 ff.

was nevertheless an essential utilitarian process, for the body would be in an extremely unwholesome condition after having been packed for several weeks in a jar of saline solution. The liquid in the jar would be turgid with fatty acids and other organic matter from the corpse, besides containing a great quantity of macerated epidermis reduced to a pulpy condition, and it would therefore be necessary to purify the body thoroughly with clean water before the ensuing stages of the embalming could be proceeded with. Dr. Blackman sees in the large jar represented in the pictures previously referred to merely a medium for collecting the lustration-water, but I believe that it actually represents the salt-bath itself, out of which the body has just been lifted, making, of course, due allowance for the conventions of Egyptian drawing. Herodotus specifically states that the body was washed *after* its immersion and *before* its wrapping in bandages. This statement, taken in conjunction with the above-mentioned lustration scenes, appears to me to lend considerable probability to my suggestion that the salting was carried out in a jar. This suggestion, moreover, would explain the significance of certain pottery figures, the meaning of which has not been understood hitherto.[1]

These figures, of which several examples are known,[1] represent a human figure in a sharply contracted attitude, sitting inside a large jar. There seems no doubt that these figures are intended to represent mummies in course of salting. It is also interesting

[1] *Proceedings of the Royal Society of Medicine*, Vol. xxi (1927), p. 847, and *Journal of Egyptian Archæology*, Vol. xiv (1928), Pl. 15.

PLATE II

POTTERY FIGURE

PROBABLY REPRESENTING A MUMMY IN COURSE OF IMMERSION IN THE SALT-BATH

to note in this connection a passage in the *Pyramid Texts* (§ 437) in which it is said that ' Unis [the king] has come forth from his jar, after having rested in his jar.' (See Plate II.)

The body having been duly salted, washed, and straightened out into a horizontal position, would consist of little more than the skin, the underlying muscular tissue, and the flesh reduced to a spongy mass, hanging loosely upon the skeleton. Whilst the body was in this pliable condition, the embalmers of the Twenty-first Dynasty, by an elaborate process which Prof. Elliot Smith has fully described,[1] packed the body under the skin with padding material, and moulded on this basis a life-like form and filled out the shrunken trunk and limbs into the plumpness they possessed during life. In the New Kingdom these modelling innovations had not been made, and such packing as the body received was done externally by padding the cavities with linen before the bandages were applied.

The next stage in the process of mummification is the most essential of all, yet it is not even mentioned by Herodotus, and is usually entirely ignored by modern writers—I refer to the desiccation of the body. Rouelle in 1754 from the examination of mummies came to the conclusion that complete desiccation had been accomplished,[2] and Rouyer in 1822, speaking of desiccation, says ' Cette opération

[1] *Contribution*, etc., *op. cit.*, *supra*, and *Annales du Service des Antiquités*, Vol. vii (1908), pp. 155 ff.

[2] G. F. Rouelle, ' Sur les Embaumements des anciens Égyptiens', *Histoire de l'Academie Royale des Sciences, année MDCCL* (Paris 1754), pp. 123–150.

dont aucun historien n'a parlé, était sans doute la principale et la plus importante de l'embaumement." [1]

A very considerable amount of heat would be necessary in order completely to desiccate the corpse when in the condition that it would assume after its long immersion in the saline bath and its subsequent washing, but we do not know by what method heat was applied, nor the extent to which sun-heat or fire-heat respectively were employed. Without complete desiccation the subsequent dressings with resin would be of little avail, and it is probably the imperfect method of drying, or the total neglect of it, that accounts for the very fragile state of most mummies embalmed before the beginning of the New Kingdom. There is reason to believe that an advanced state of efficiency had been reached by the embalmers of the Pyramid Age (Dynasties IV–VI), and that thereafter the art deteriorated and was only made thoroughly efficient in the Eighteenth Dynasty. It seems unlikely that sun-heat alone could be the only medium for desiccation. The atmospheric conditions of the country and the abundance of insects would rather tend to the destruction than the preservation of a body exposed to their influence, and it therefore seems probable that fire-heat was used, through the medium of some apparatus of which we at present have no information. A discovery made in the season 1924–5 in a Theban tomb by Mr. S. Yeivin, excavating for Mr. Robert Mond, is interesting and suggestive in this connection. In some of the chambers of the

[1] P. C. Rouyer, 'Notice sur les Embaumements' in the *Description de l'Egypte*, 2nd ed., t. vi, Antiquités, Mémoires (Paris 1822), pp. 461–489.

tomb 'a vast number of dried mummies were piled up almost to the ceiling in a state of disorder. . . . The mummies, to judge from their appearance, seem to have been dried over a slow fire, which would explain the smoky appearance of all the chambers and passages above.' [1] From this it would appear that a chamber in an old and disused tomb had been utilized in later times as a convenient place in which to desiccate mummies. Many tombs in Egypt bear evidence of having been the scene of fire. The blackened ceilings and walls, with damage to the plaster and chemical changes in the colouring matter used for decorative purposes, and the above instance, may give a hint as to how they came to be in this condition. The above points are to be taken as no more than mere suggestions, for until the mummies have been minutely examined no definite evidence can be afforded by them.

However it may have been accomplished, the body was dried, and was then rendered more or less supple by a liberal application of a paste consisting of resin, mixed with natron or salt, and animal fat. In later times unmixed resin seems to have been used, and to have been poured into and over the body in a molten condition. Possibly also fire-heat was used to render the stream of resin more mobile, for it penetrates into every cavity and crevice, and even into the structure of the bones. I may take this opportunity of saying that bitumen, although described in modern books as the staple embalming material, was apparently never used, for modern chemical

[1] S. Yeivin, *Annals of Archæology and Anthropology*, Vol. xiii (1926), p. 15.

analysis has failed to discover its presence in numerous specimens examined. The material is actually resin, and the lustrous black surface with which it dries has apparently deceived both ancient and modern observers. The resinous paste used by the embalmers of the New Kingdom was heated in order to render it freely liquid, and into it balls and wads of linen were dipped, and these were packed into the vacant body-cavity.[1] The edges of the embalming-wound were then brought into apposition, and covered by a metal or wax plate, usually engraved with the symbolic eye. This plate required no fixing, for it became embedded in the thick coat of resinous paste with which the body was smeared. Occasionally the wound was sewn up by a running suture of string or a thin band of linen, but this practice was seldom resorted to, and in such cases no wax plate was used.[2] The cranium was next packed with strips of linen dipped in resin, and the nostrils similarly plugged, their orifices often being closed by a lump of resin or wax pushed into the fossæ. The body and limbs were then treated with more resinous paste, and the trunk and limbs separately swathed. After each had received several layers of bandage, the arms were arranged in position, either crossed on the breast or extended by the side of the trunk (the positions varied from time to time) and the wrapping then

[1] In the Twenty-first Dynasty the viscera were separately embalmed and wrapped in linen parcels and restored to the body-cavity. Such free space as remained was filled with packing material.

[2] Examples in Dynasties XVIII–XX are the mummies of Thuiu and of the Pharaohs, Siptah, Sety II and Rameses IV.

proceeded over the whole, body and limbs together. During the anointing and bandaging processes, a priest recited from a service book the appropriate liturgy.

In two of the Theban tombs (and possibly more) pictures of bandaging the mummy have survived. In that of Thoy (see Plate III, *a*) are four badly damaged scenes each of which represents an episode in the ritual of embalming. The theatre of operations is the embalmer's workshop, the door of which, following the usual convention, is shown on the left side of each picture. The mummy lies extended, and is supported upon two blocks or pedestals, and two men, one at the head the other at the foot, proceed with its toilet. Between the mummy and the door stands a priest holding a papyrus and making ceremonial gestures. In the first scene the operators have their hands extended over the mummy, apparently adjusting its bandages. The inscription is too fragmentary to enlighten us, but the remains of the determinative show that it was concerned in some way with cloth and refers to the bandages. In the second picture, one of the operators is kneeling, but the scene is so mutilated, that little can be learned from it. The third picture is more complete, and gives some interesting details. Herodotus tells us that the linen bandages were smeared with 'gum', and here we see the two operators actually applying this 'gum' (resin) to the bandages. Each holds a saucer in one hand, and with the other applies the liquid with a brush. Under the mummy is a large two-handled pan from which they replenish their saucers, and over the door is a similar pan

heating upon a stove or brazier to replace the first
pan when empty. The examination of mummies
themselves makes it quite evident that the resinous
paste was applied to the body and to the bandages
hot, and it is interesting to find this confirmation.
The Rhind Papyri also state that the paste was
heated.[1] The text when complete described the
picture, and just sufficient of it remains to read
' applying the paste '. The fourth scene is too badly
damaged to give us any information, but it is evident
that further bandages are being applied, as a chest
or coffer now replaces the brazier of the former scene.
In another tomb, that of Amenemope (Pl. III, b), a
very similar series of scenes, six in number, formerly
existed. A copy made by Rosellini a century ago
has fortunately been preserved, for the picture is
to-day almost entirely destroyed. The first scene
shows the brazier and the application of hot resin, as
in the other tomb, and the others represent the
bandaging of the mummy, the decoration of the
cartonage mask and other objects connected with the
embalming. The fifth scene is of particular interest.
The rectangular object over the head of the seated
man on the right, seems to be the board with its
transverse bars upon which the mummy was laid
when the first operations were performed upon it.
The seated man cleaning out a large jar may have
in his hands either the jar in which the salting was
carried out, or else one of the jars in which the
embalming materials were stowed after the process
had been completed. All the materials used, including
the soiled linen and surplus drugs, were carefully

---

[1] *Papyrus Rhind No.* 1, p. 3, line 6 ; *No.* 2, p. 4, line 3.

PLATE III

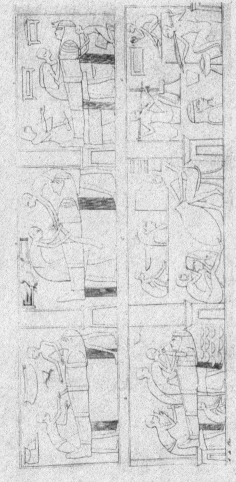

(a) Tomb of Thoy. *Drawn from a photograph of the original*

(b) Tomb of Amenemope. *After the drawing made by Rosellini, about 1829*

EGYPTIAN EMBALMERS: WALL-PAINTINGS FROM THEBAN TOMBS OF THE XIXth DYNASTY

packed into jars, and placed in the tomb or in a small chamber or pit near it.[1] Occasionally these materials were put into a coffin,[2] such was the respect with which they were treated, for it must not be forgotten that the whole process of mummification, apart from its avowed physical purpose of preserving the body from decay, was a religious ceremony closely connected with the cult of Osiris.

It is not necessary to describe in detail the treatment of the organs that were removed from the body. It is not known what was done with the brain ; Herodotus does not refer to it, and it is probable that it was treated as waste, for it must have been removed in very small fragments through the nose. The viscera were wrapped into four parcels and each parcel was placed, under the protection of one of the Four Sons of Horus, in an appropriate Canopic jar. These jars have been found of all periods from the Fourth Dynasty onwards. During the Twenty-first and Twenty-second Dynasties the practice of placing the viscera in Canopic jars was given up, and they were wrapped in four parcels, each with a wax image of its appropriate guardian deity, and returned to the body. Canopic jars of this period are known, but they are dummies, and figure amongst the burial equipment merely in servile obedience to the old tradition. The use of Canopic jars was revived during the Saïte period, but at that time an alternative method of disposing of the viscera was introduced,

[1] Several such dumps of embalming materials have been discovered in recent years.
[2] E. Naville, *Deir el Bahari*, Part ii (London 1897) p. 6; Winlock, *op. cit.*, 1922, fig. 30 and p. 32.

for they were often covered with spices and placed between the legs of the mummy.

The general method of mummification summarily described above was not the only one in use, for mummies have been found without embalming-wounds, and these were either eviscerated *per anum*, or were not eviscerated at all. Herodotus' 'second method', that of removing the viscera in a fluid state by means of cedar oil, is not possible as he states it ; but the injection of a corrosive or astringent fluid might have arrested decomposition until the body was ready for desiccation. In certain cases some of the viscera were actually excised *per anum*, and in others no attempt at all had been made to remove them. I recently examined two well-preserved mummies of the Twenty-sixth Dynasty which had been neither eviscerated nor immersed in a salt-bath, yet both were in an excellent state of preservation. There was no embalming-wound, nor had the anal method been resorted to. The epidermis was intact, and all the body-hair was present, for it happens that these mummies were both of muscular men, with abundant hair on the chest and limbs. The nails were *in situ*, and had not been artificially attached. The bodies had been merely desiccated, then covered with a liberal supply of resinous paste in which numerous white crystals can be seen.[1] The skin is soft and flexible, and the bodies do not show the considerable shrinking which inevitably occurs whenever the salt-bath has been used.

[1] This efflorescence may have been fatty acids. See A. Lucas, *Preservative Materials used in Embalming* (Cairo 1911), p. 35.

Another method of preservation was to sprinkle the body after desiccation with crude natron. This has a corrosive effect on the bandages nearest to the body, which often present the appearance of having been scorched or burnt. This sprinkling with natron was common in the New Kingdom and was probably intended to absorb any moisture which might exude from the body or from the paste with which it was coated.

The application of the bandages was a long and complicated process. The *Ritual of Embalming* gives directions for anointing and bandaging the head, back, hands and legs. The bandages all had magical names, and as each was applied a long utterance was recited by the priest. According to this text, many of the bandages were inscribed with their names or had drawings traced upon them. So far as I am aware, the only attempt hitherto made to verify the particulars of the Ritual by observation of the bandaging of actual mummies is that made many years ago by the late Professor Macalister, but as the mummies he examined were of various dates, and little was known as to their age or provenance, he did not obtain any useful results.[1]

The value of the custom of mummification to the development of anatomical knowledge will be discussed in Chapter VI.

[1] *Journal of the Anthropological Inst.*, Vol. xxxvi (1893), pp. 161 ff.

CHAPTER IV

MAGICIANS AND POSSESSING SPIRITS

DEATH was not the only accident that befell unwary men: illness and disease had also to be reckoned with, and as their cause was impalpable and invisible, it was ever laid at the door of supernatural influence. To-day the belief is widespread that illness is caused by sorcery, witchcraft, or by evil spirits. Every healthy man was ever liable to fall a prey to such powers, and elaborate measures were taken to protect the living from possession, just as they were to protect the dead from extinction.

The present-day belief in possession as a cause of illness amongst primitive peoples echoes, as has already been remarked, the same ancient belief that is clearly expressed in the earliest magical and medical literature that has survived the Egyptian medical texts. In tracing the history of medicine we must naturally base our researches upon the oldest materials available, and consequently Egyptian medicine is the foundation upon which the structure of a great science has been erected, because it antedates the earliest medical records of other countries by many centuries.

As will appear more fully in a later chapter, there cannot be the slightest doubt that medicine had its origin in magic, and that for many centuries—almost

52

to the present day, in fact—magic has never completely lost its hold on medicine.   The earliest doctors
were accordingly magicians, and the earliest forms of
medical treatment were magical rites.   The intimate
connection between magic and religion is clearly shown
in the fact that the first magicians of which we have
any record were priests, and throughout Egyptian history many of the functions of the priesthood were
magical in character.   The magician's functions were
numerous : in addition to his religious duties, he was
called into request by many contingencies,[1] such, for
instance, as identifying criminals, and sometimes he
appears as a wonder-worker for the amusement of the
king and his court.

A document now in the Berlin Museum, known as
the Westcar Papyrus, contains a series of popular
stories of the wonders worked for the entertainment
of the Pharaohs of the Pyramid age.   In these narra-
tives we are told of a magician who fashioned a
miniature crocodile of wax over which he recited
magical spells and transformed it into a full-grown
live crocodile which seized a guilty man.   In another
episode, the magician parted the waters of a lake in
order to recover from its bed a jewel that had been
dropped into the water from a boat.   King Cheops,
the builder of the Great Pyramid, was entertained by
the prodigies worked by a magician named Dedi,
who was a most remarkable person.   The text says
of him : ' There is a man of humble birth and Dedi
is his name.   He is a poor man a hundred and ten years

[1] See A. H. Gardiner, ' Professional Magicians in Ancient
Egypt', *Proceedings of the Society of Biblical Archæology*, Vol.
xxxix (1917), pp. 31–44.

old, yet he can eat five loaves of bread, a haunch of beef, and can drink a hundred jugs of beer at this very day.'

The King on hearing this, was anxious to see this Dedi, and he sent his son to escort the old man to his palace. The magician, though a poor man, lived in some luxury, for the prince found him enjoying a siesta outside his door : ' he found him lying on a couch at the door of his house, a servant was stroking his head for him, and another was tickling the soles of his feet'. The prince conducted the old man to the court, where he was greeted by the king, who said : ' Is it true, as it is rumoured, that thou canst put on a head that has been cut off ? ' Dedi answered in the affirmative, and the king ordered a prisoner to be brought in and beheaded in order that Dedi might give proof of his powers. The magician, however, refused to experiment on a human subject, and asked for a goose instead. The bird was accordingly brought, and its head chopped off, ' and the goose was put on the left side of the chamber, and its head on the right side of the chamber. And Dedi recited his magic spells, at which the goose arose and moved, and its head also. Now when the one had reached the other, the goose stood up and cackled.' Similar experiments were performed with a duck and with an ox.[1]

The stories of these wonderful magicians of ancient times were current in Egypt for many years after the time at which they lived. It is, however, as a healer or preventer of disease, rather than as a mere

[1] For the stories of magicians in the Westcar Papyrus, see G. Maspero, *Popular Stories of Ancient Egypt* (London 1915), pp. 21–42 ; A. Erman, *The Literature of the Ancient Egyptians* [transl. by A. M. Blackman], (London 1927), pp. 36–47.

wonder-worker that the magician is most often met
with. It is known how he operated in such cases,
for a large number of magical papyri has been found
in Egypt, now preserved in various museums, in
which are set out at length the spells and incantations
the magician uttered, and minute directions as to
how he should proceed in various cases. In these
papyri the idea of possession is very evident, for
diseases and illnesses are treated as if personified,
and they are addressed and harangued by the magician.
Usually the sickness, personified, is addressed by the
magician, but sometimes he calls upon the poison
or other influence that it was believed to have pro-
jected into the patient's body.

The simplest method of treatment was the recitation of a spell in which the demon was simply com-
manded to quit, or the poison to leave the patient's
body. Such spells are usually full of references to
the gods, and the defeat of the demon is generally
attributed to their power, or rather to the mystic
force inherent in their names. It was important,
also, that the patient's name should be uttered in
the spell, in order that the possessing spirit might
clearly understand that its presence in the body of
such and such a specific victim was being referred to
by the magician. Accordingly in the written spells
a place is always indicated at which the patient's
name should be mentioned. The formula in Egyptian
is ' so and so, born of so and so (fem.) ', or, as the
French equivalent better expresses it, ' un tel, né
d'une telle '. Many examples of such spells might be
quoted :[1] they begin by warning the demon off, and

1 Some specimens are given below (see pp. 56, 72, etc.).

continue by informing it of its powerlessness to exert
evil influence when under the magician's ban. 'Get
thee back thou enemy, thou dead man or dead
woman who dost cause pain to M born of N. . . .
Thy arms have no power over his arms, thy legs have
no power over his legs. No limbs of thine have
power over any limbs of his,' etc.[1] A fuller spell, in
which the magician assumes the rôle of Horus, will
give a good idea of the nature of these utterances.

'Flow out, thou poison, come forth upon the ground.
Horus conjures thee, he cuts thee off, he spits thee out, and
thou risest not up but fallest down. Thou art weak and not
strong, a coward and dost not fight, blind and dost not see.
Thou liftest not thy face. Thou art turned back and findest
not the way. Thou mournest and dost not rejoice. Thou
creepest away and dost not appear. So speaketh Horus,
efficacious in magic ! The poison which was rejoicing the
hearts of multitudes grieve for it : Horus has slain it by his
magic. He who mourned is in joy. Stand up thou who
was prostrate, Horus has restored thee to life. He who came
as one carried is gone forth as himself : Horus has overcome
his bites. All men when they behold Rē, praise the son of
Osiris. Turn back, thou snake, conjured is thy poison which
was in any limb of N the son of M. Behold the magic of
Horus is powerful against thee. Flow out, thou poison, come
forth upon the ground.'[2]

The mere word of the magician, or the mere mention
of the name of a god is often alone considered as
marking the demon's defeat. 'Thou fliest before the

---

[1] A. H. Gardiner, *Theban Ostraka* (Toronto and Oxford
1913), p. 14. [The above is not a verbal quotation.]

[2] A. H. Gardiner, art. 'Magic (Egyptian)' in *Hastings'
Encyclopædia of Religion and Ethics*, Vol. viii (Edinburgh
1915), p. 264.

sorcerer, before the servant of Horus, as soon as he mentions the name of Horus, or the name of Seth, the lord of heaven. . . . So dost thou die, and the report goes forth to the house of Rē that Horus has conquered the disease.' [1]

Treatment of this kind was usually effected by word of mouth only. In most spells, however, the spoken word is accompanied by gestures, or by the use of figures, amulets or other substances which the magician charges with occult power. These two phases of the magician's art have been aptly defined by Dr. Alan Gardiner as the *oral rite* and the *manual rite* respectively. It is usual in the magical texts, to find a rubric at the end of the oral rite giving directions as to the accompanying manual rite. ' Say the words four times over a cord in which seven knots have been tied,' is a frequent rubric of this kind, and many variant forms of it occur. Thus at the end of a spell to assuage the pains of labour and to facilitate birth is the rubric : ' Say the words four times over a dwarf of clay to be placed upon the forehead of the woman who is giving birth.' [2] Often the manual rite took the form of giving the patient mixtures of various substances to eat or drink. The dose so given was rendered efficacious by reciting over it a spell or incantation. The Ebers Papyrus, for instance, begins with a long incantation which is intended to give efficacy to the numerous prescriptions that follow.[3] In my opinion the prescriptions in the

[1] *Leiden Papyrus*, I, 345, Recto, G. iii, ii–G. iv, 1 ; Gardiner, *loc. cit.*

[2] *Leiden Papyrus*, I, 348, 12, 6.

[3] *Ebers Papyrus*, i, 1–2, 6. See below, p. 71.

medical papyri are but elaborations of the manual rite of the magician, and it is for this reason that the papyri are interspersed with magical spells that constitute the oral rites belonging to each group of prescriptions that follows and that are recited by the magician in order to make the doses effective. Many of the doses contain foul or offensive substances, and the object of these is obviously to be as unpalatable as possible to the possessing spirit, so as to give it no encouragement to linger in the patient's body. But even wholesome drugs could be offensive to spirits. Thus in one of the spells it is said to the demon : ' I make a charm for him against thee with the *efai*-plant which injures ; with onions which destroy thee ; and with honey which is sweet to the living and bitter to the dead.' [1] In this case it is the spirit of a dead man that possesses the patient and makes him ill.

It is characteristic of the magician at all times that he should have more than one string to his bow, for if one remedy fails, another may succeed, and his reputation must at all costs be maintained. Consequently in the medical papyri are found numerous alternative prescriptions for each ailment and in the magical texts alternative spells provided for every kind of sickness or calamity. Some of these remedies contain drugs that are really beneficial and appropriate, and such prescriptions, actually accomplishing their purpose, would tend to survive their more fantastic fellows. By such means, more and more reliance came to be placed upon the drugs themselves, and

---

[1] *Berlin Papyrus*, 3027, 2, 4. In this spell the word ' onion ' puns on that for ' destroy '.

less upon the magician's spells, and the persons therefore who would be most in request in cases of sickness would be those who were skilled in the knowledge
and preparation of drugs. Such men were no longer
magicians, but physicians.

It must not be supposed that the coming of the
physician extinguished magic. It is rare in human
experience for the new completely to supersede the
old. This fact, indeed, could be abundantly illus-
trated from the events of our life to-day. We still
perpetuate countless ceremonies and customs that
have entirely lost their significance : in coronation
ritual, in numerous civic functions, at the launching
of ships, at births, deaths and marriages, and on
scores of other occasions. The old forms, stripped of
their significance, continue in their places beside the
new, but perhaps they were originally conserved as a
reserve for emergencies ; and just as the first steam-
boats were provided with auxiliary sails, so the first
physicians kept magic as a stand-by to be used in
case of need. Medicine branched off from magic and
began its independent career early in Egyptian history,
for already in the Pyramid Age there are records of
men bearing the title of physician as distinct from
magician. But even the physicians were closely
associated with magic and with religion, and magical
and religious elements continued to pervade medicine.
Both medicine and magic were 'mysteries' and a
knowledge of them implied special powers on the
part of their exponents. There is, in the necropolis
of Sakkara, the tomb of an eminent man who lived
in the Pyramid Age. Amongst his titles, which
include 'priest of Selkis' (a goddess particularly

associated with magic) there is also ' Royal Physician, interpreter of a difficult science '. [1]

The religious element in medicine is evident from the fact that every part of the body was associated with a god or a goddess. There are extant many lists of the organs of the body, both internal and external, with the names of the divinities to whose protection they were ascribed. These lists are found in documents of all periods from the Pyramid texts of the Fifth and Sixth Dynasties to the end of Egyptian independence in the Thirtieth. On the walls of the Pyramids of Sakkara,[2] in the Book of the Dead,[3] in the long texts inscribed on the wooden coffins of the Middle Kingdom,[4] in the magical papyri of the New Kingdom (as exemplified by those in the museums of Berlin, Leiden, Turin and Rome [5]), in the inscriptions engraved on the walls of the royal tombs at Thebes,[6] in the great Metternich stele of the Thirtieth Dynasty and elsewhere,[7] such lists of organs

---

[1] J. E. Quibell, *Excavations at Saqqara in* 1905–6 (Cairo 1907), p. 22 ; T. E. Peet, *Proc. Society of Biblical Archæology*, Vol. xxxvii (1915), p. 224.

[2] *Pyramid Texts*, §§ 1303–1315.   [3] *Book of the Dead*, § 42.

[4] S. Birch, *Egyptian Texts from the Coffin of Amamu* (London 1886), Pl. xxiv, 11–18 ; P. Lacau, *Textes Religieux* (Paris 1910), No. xxvii, p. 76.

[5] *Berlin Papyrus*, 3027, Recto, 3, 6–5, 5 ; Verso, 4, 8–5, 5 ; *Leiden Papyrus*, I, 348, Verso, 5, 1–6, 1 ; *Turin Papyrus*, 125, 5 ff. ; *Vatican Papyrus, No.* 36.

[6] Those of Sety I, Meneptah and Sety II. E. Naville, *La Litanie du Soleil* (Leipsic 1875), Pls. 14, 20, 21, 32.

[7] W. Golenischeff, *Die Metternichstele* (Leipsic 1877), Pl. ii, lines 15–32. A still later list of parts of the body, in a Ptolemaic inscription, has recently been published by E. Drioton, *Revue de l'Egypte Ancienne*, t. i (Paris 1927), pp. 134–136.

tabulated with the names of their tutelary deities are to be found. In some documents, such as the Berlin Papyrus that contains spells and prescriptions for mothers and their new-born babes, there are two such lists, one containing thirty-six and the other twenty-three different organs or parts of the body. These lists usually end with the phrase 'there is no part of the body without its god'. With this custom of placing the parts of the body under divine protection, may be compared that of later times in which each region of the body was placed under the influence of one of the signs of the zodiac. The religious element again appears in a series of prescriptions in the Ebers and Hearst Papyri, each of which is claimed to have been invented by a god. Thus there is 'a prescription which Rē made on his own behalf', 'a second prescription which Shu made on his own behalf', 'a third prescription which Tefnut made on behalf of Rē', and so on.[1] In a later chapter examination will be made of Egyptian medicine as apart from magic, but concerning the latter a few more words may be said. Attention has already been called to the close relationship between magic and medicine, and in this connection it may be noted that Dr. Alan Gardiner has admirably summarized the relationship when he said, 'Medical books are seldom free from incantations, and the magical papyri are leavened with medical prescriptions'.[2]

Apart from diseases and evil spirits that were treated as personified by the magicians, magic itself

[1] *Ebers Papyrus*, 46, 16–47, 10 ; *Hearst Papyrus*, 5, 7–15.
[2] Art. 'Magic (Egyptian)' in *Hastings' Encyclopædia of Religion and Ethics*, Vol. viii (Edinburgh 1915), p. 267.

was sometimes believed to be the cause of illness. There is a collection of prescriptions headed 'to banish magic from the body'.[1] Other ailments, as already noted, were laid to the charge of a god, a goddess, an enemy, a dead man or a dead woman. Spirits of foreign origin were especially formidable, and there are formulæ for repelling the 'influence' of a negress or of an 'Asiatic woman who steals in secretly in the dark'.[2] The possessing spirit either resided in the patient's body or else injected into it some poison or other hurtful influence. Once installed, the demon or its influence made the patient ill, and the speedy rejection of the demon was necessary. This was accomplished by the spells to which reference has already been made, by the use of amulets, or by the administration of a dose, or by these various methods combined. The ejected spirit left the patient's body in various ways : either it came out through the excretions of the body, the fæces, the urine or sweat,[3] or it passed out in wind.[4] Sometimes however such natural channels of exit were not used, but the magician called upon the affected parts of the body to 'open their mouths' and disgorge what was within them,[5] which seems to imply the belief that the magician could make a fortuitous opening in the body for the purpose of ridding it of its possessing

[1] *Ebers Papyrus*, 34, 2–35, 12.

[2] *Berlin Papyrus*, 3027, 2, 7.

[3] *Berlin Papyrus*, 3027, 2, 8–10. Here the demon's influence is bidden to come out through the secretions of the nose or the sweat of the body.

[4] *Leiden Papyrus*, I. 348, Verso, 12, 9, 'it comes forth as flatus from his anus.'

[5] *Leiden Papyrus*, I. 345, Verso, G. ii, 14.

influence.   In the medical papyri each prescription is
headed by a title (always written in red), and instead
of the simple phrase 'prescription for curing' such
and such a disease, we find the words 'prescription
for banishing', 'driving out', 'terrifying' or 'killing'
the disease.   In such phraseology the idea of possession is manifest.   Some of the prescriptions, however,
are for 'treating' a disease : these must be regarded
as later in origin than the others, and were introduced at the period when the manual rite was super-
seding in importance the oral rite, that is to say, when
rational therapeutics began to take the place of pure
magic.   The notion of possession is never entirely
absent, however, and even when treating a disease by
rational therapeutic methods, the physician could
never forget that his craft originated in various
attempts to coax, charm or forcibly expel the disease-
causing demon from its involuntary host.   Indeed
many of the drugs in the medical papyri, even when
wholesome and rational, originally found their way
into the pharmacopœia for purely magical reasons.
There seems to me to be abundant evidence that their
choice was not originally dictated by reason, knowledge or experience.   It is true that we are ignorant
of the origin of most of the drugs used, but it is
known that in many cases substances were employed
simply because their names made puns upon certain
words in the recited incantations and for other similar
reasons.[1]   As has already been noted, many alternative prescriptions are given for each complaint,

[1] Throughout Egyptian literature, both secular and
religious, the Egyptians lost no opportunity of making plays
on words, a habit that frequently led to the introduction of

and these contain elements whose actions, if any, are often widely different from one another. The very multiplicity of prescriptions is of itself a confession of their purely arbitrary and unscientific character. Now it sometimes happened that one or more of the drugs contained in the various prescriptions really did accomplish the end for which it was employed, and consequently such remedies of known efficacy would acquire a reputation and tend to supersede the purely arbitrary and useless elements. Herein lies the real beginning of pharmacy. Its origin is somewhat analogous to Charles Lamb's famous story of roast pork, but before it could be definitely known that such and such a herb really had such and such a property, many generations of sufferers must have had to submit to the arbitrary and often nauseating doses that contained nothing beneficial and that must at times have been positively harmful. Such a course of semi-ineffectual experimenting was the necessary forerunner of any attempt to classify drugs and to record the purposes for which each was best suited. In such an attempted classification the Herbal had its birth.[1]

It has already been stated, and must be repeated, that the gradual infiltration of rationalism into medical practice did not by any means give a death-blow to magic. Magical methods continued to be employed side by side with more rational procedure, as the

periphrases simply to make puns. Many instances of the punning of words in prescriptions and incantations might be quoted. See Gardiner, *op. cit., supra*, pp. 265–267.

[1] I have dealt fully with this question in a memoir to be published in *Ægyptus*, Vol. x.

medical papyri of Pharaonic times plainly show. Moreover, the existence of numerous papyri, dating from Ptolemaic times and later, written in demotic Egyptian, Greek and Coptic, show that magical practices for the cure of disease were in active operation long after the influence of scientific medicine, that was mainly due to the Greeks, had made itself felt. Magic maintained full sway throughout the Dark Ages and the Middle Ages: it persisted into the sixteenth, seventeenth and eighteenth centuries, and it is not yet wholly extinct. The magician, when he had become physician, was loth to part with the mysticism of his craft, and he often disguised his more rational forms of treatment under a veneer of mystery. There was always a preference for rare and bizarre elements in the prescriptions of drugs. This combination of magical and rational methods is well shown in the large group of prescriptions for treating stiff joints, muscular complaints and rheumatoid troubles.[1] These mostly consist of ointments and emollients, the basis of which is a grease made of animal fat. So far, this is quite appropriate and rational. The magical element appears when, instead of merely ox-fat or goose-grease, the prescriptions introduce the fat of all kinds of different animals, many of them rare and difficult to obtain, such as the lion, oryx, hippopotamus, snake, lizard, mouse, etc. Similarly in a prescription for an ointment for the scalp we find:

' Fat of a lion, 1 [part]; fat of a hippopotamus, 1; fat of a crocodile, 1; fat of a cat, 1; fat of a snake, 1; fat of an ibex, 1. Mix into one mass; anoint the head therewith.' [2]

---

[1] There are many of these in the Ebers, Hearst, and Berlin medical papyri.   [2] *Ebers Papyrus*, 66, 9-12.

The combination of the fats of all these different animals was clearly dictated by a belief in their respective magical virtues, and is not controlled merely by the rationalistic use of grease as an ointment. The magicians, moreover, had an interested motive in ascribing virtues to substances difficult for the patient to obtain. No patient could on the spur of the moment possess himself of the fats of all these animals, but he could purchase from his healer a series of gallipots each respectively labelled as the fat of such and such an animal, whilst the pots actually contained, probably each and all of them, nothing but the homely goose-grease with perhaps a little colouring-matter added, and bearing an appropriate label !

Even diseases that have obvious external manifestations such as boils, sores or swellings, were believed to be caused by possessing spirits : at first wounds alone, because inflicted by visible human agency and therefore material and comprehensible, were treated by rational and practical means, and the analogies in the morbid conditions associated with or resulting from wounds, such as suppuration, swelling and other manifestations, led the physicians to become surgeons and to apply similar rational methods of treatment to morbid conditions arising from disease.

It does not in the least prejudice the view here expressed that possession was originally believed to be the cause of illness, that many of the prescriptions in the medical papyri are for the treatment of affections in various named organs of the body. This fact merely shows that in many cases the Egyptians were able to localize the seat of the trouble, but it does not remove the belief that spirits were the cause of the mischief. Demons fear amulets, and for this reason knotted cords, images or other objects were often placed on the affected part. Sometimes, however, instead of being thus locally applied, these charms were merely hung round the neck, or, again to increase the mystic element, they might be attached to some part of the body far removed from the seat of the trouble. Thus an amulet used in connection with certain spells for the cure of headache is to be tied to the patient's left foot,[1] or to his big toe,[2] and in a prescription of drugs for an ailment of the eye, directions are given to apply the preparation to the patient's ear.[3] The knotted cords, to which reference has already been made (usually having *seven* knots in them),[4] were very frequently used, not only in Egypt, but in many other lands. The knots were evidently believed to be magical barriers that impeded the passage of malign influences into the body. In one of the Turin papyri there is an utterance that clearly illustrates this idea: ' If the poison pass these seven knots which Horus has made on his body, I will not allow the sun to shine.' [5] Sometimes the knots were each identified with a god, who, if properly propitiated, stationed himself, so to speak, at his knot on the magic cord, and thus acted as a sort of door-keeper to ward off evil influence.

[1] *Leiden Papyrus*, I. 348, Verso, 4, 3.   [2] *Ibid.*, 3, 1.
[3] *Ebers Papyrus*, 57, 19.
[4] In a paper on the magical significance of the number *seven* I have collected many instances. *Ægyptus*, Vol. viii (Milan 1927), pp. 97–107.   [5] Gardiner, *op. cit., supra*, p. 266.

6

The latter part of the spell just quoted illustrates another feature of these magical utterances. The magician claims a power over the elements and threatens to suspend the forces of nature if his commands are disobeyed by the demon he is exorcising. The threats are often very daring and are directed against the gods themselves. In a spell against scorpion-stings the magician threatens to stop the flow of the Nile, the light of the sun and the growth of seeds, if Selkis, the scorpion-goddess, dares to sting his client. At times he even threatens to cast fire into the shrine of Osiris and burn up the god![1] In the Pyramid Texts dire threats are uttered against the gods by the king who is addressing them, but at the end of his harangue, the speaker, fearing that he has become too bold, disclaims responsibility for his words and lays the responsibility on divine shoulders : ' It is not this Pepi [the king] who says this against you, ye gods : it is Hikē [the god of magic] who says this against you, ye gods.'[2]

The gods are thus made the scapegoats of the magician when his menaces have overstepped the bounds of prudence. By the frequent habit of impersonating the gods, the magician also claimed indemnity against the results of his utterances. Many spells begin with the words : ' I am Rē ', ' I am Horus ', etc.

A method of destroying hostile powers that was practised in ancient Egypt and is widespread at the

[1] Spells in a papyrus at Turin. Cf. Gardiner, *op. cit.*, p. 265.
[2] *Pyramid Texts*, § 1324. Similar disclaimers occur in the magical papyri, where the blame is laid upon the goddess Isis, e.g. *Leiden Pap.*, I. 348, 11, 7 ; *Turin, Pap.*, 136, 8–9 ; *Harris Magical Papyrus*, 9, 11.

present day, was the making of wax effigies of the demons or the drawing of pictures of them. The effigies or pictures were burnt, and by sympathetic magic the demons inherent in them were believed to be consumed by the flames. Sickness, disease or poison were generally treated by the magician as personified, and other influences were dealt with in the same way. Thus spells were recited for inducing dreams,[1] for 'repelling fear that comes to befall a man by day or by night from before or behind ',[2] or for averting anger.[3] Burns were treated, not only by drugs, but by incantations,[4] as were also the bites of snakes and the stings of scorpions.[5]

Before leaving the magician and his spells, reference may be made to a few further specimens of magical utterance. It will first be convenient to call attention to the distinctive names that the Egyptians gave to the various formulæ in which the magical and medical texts are framed. These are :—

(i) , *ro*, ' spell '. This is the general name given to magical utterances, usually of a defensive or protective kind. The *Book of the Dead* is made up almost entirely of a collection of *ro*, or spells for procuring for the dead protection from danger and happiness after death.

---

[1] *Louvre Papyrus*, 3229.
[2] *Leiden Papyrus*, I. 348, 2, 1–7.
[3] *London-Leiden Magical Papyrus*, 15, 24–31.
[4] A passage in *Leiden Papyrus*. I. 348 (3, 1 ff.) is headed ' Beginning of the Incantations for burns.'
[5] *Turin Papyri*, often, and *Leiden Papyrus*, I. 349.

(ii)   _shĭnet_, 'incantation'. Most of the long magical incantations, in which the oral rite is more prominent than the manual rite, are called by this name.

(iii)   _s'a_, 'charm'. A title often given to spells of protective magic.

(iv)   _pakhret_, 'prescription'. This is the usual title for a collection of drugs administered as the manual rite.

(v)   _sep_, 'dose'. A word used also for prescriptions of drugs.

(vi)   _shes'aw_, 'directions'. This word is used as a heading for the cases that are diagnosed and that contain definite instructions as to procedure. It is used in the title for all the cases in the Edwin Smith Papyrus, for most of those in the Kahun Papyrus, and in certain sections of the Ebers Papyrus.

The following spell introduces the oral and manual rites, and is a good specimen of an incantation of protective magic. It is uttered for the welfare of a new-born child:

'Greeting to you! Isis hath twined and Nephthys hath tied the knot of the divine cord of seven knots with which I protect thee, O hale child, N born of M, that thou mayest be healthy; that thou mayest thrive; that thou mayest satisfy every god and every goddess; that every male enemy who shall traverse thy path may be overthrown; and that every female enemy who shall traverse thy path may be overthrown ; that every mouth that maligns thee may be stopped-up [lit. " walled up "], as the mouths are stopped-up and as the mouths are sealed of the 770 asses that are in the Lake of Desdes [a mythological locality].   I know them : I know their names, but he that knows them not and would plan evil against this child, would suffer repulse nevertheless.   This spell is to be recited over seven beads of porphyry, seven beads of gold, seven threads of flax threaded by the two sister-mothers [i.e. Isis and Nephthys], one of whom threads, the other ties them.   To be completed by seven knots therein, and put upon the neck of this child.' [1]

The Ebers Papyrus opens with a series of spells (*ro*) intended to give efficacy to the numerous prescriptions (*pakhret*) that follow.   The first of these is headed : ' Beginning of the spells for placing the prescription upon any member of a man '.   This is evidently intended for external medicines.   It ends with the formula : ' Say the words when placing the prescription upon every member of the man that suffers '.   The second is also for external treatment, and the third is for a medicine that is swallowed. Its title is : ' Spell for drinking a prescription '; it then proceeds, ' Welcome prescription !   Welcome ! that dost drive away that which is in this my heart and in these my limbs.   Hikē [the god of magic] is victorious in the prescription ! '   The text then proceeds with an allusion to the mythological combat between Horus and Seth.   It ends with the formula : ' Say the words when drinking the medicine : a true remedy a million times ! ' [2]

Finally, here is a spell taken from a long series of

[1] *Berlin Papyrus*, 3027, Verso, 6, 1–7.
[2] *Ebers Papyrus*, 2, 1–6.

utterances whose object is to drive away affections
of the head, probably headache:

'O enemy, male or female! O dead, male or female!
O adversary, male or female! Descend not upon the head
of M, the son of N, for [his head] is the head of Rē himself
which illumines the earth and gives life to mortals! Beware
lest Rē goeth to rest hungry! Beware lest the gods suffer,
for then will darkness fall, clouds will obscure the sky, and
water shall o'erspread the earth!'[1]

Leave must now be taken of the magician and
some consideration given to the development of
medicine when it begins to outgrow its magical in-
fancy and to emerge into its adolescence of rationalism.

[1] *Leiden Papyrus* I., 348, Verso, 4, 3-5.

CHAPTER V

THE BEGINNINGS OF THERAPEUTICS AND SURGERY. THE FIRST MEDICAL BOOKS

SOME account has already been given of the *modus operandi* of the magician. His principal medium was the employment of oral and manual rites, and it was the development of the manual rite that first called the doctor into existence. For when the rite took the form of administering to the patient—either for the sufferer's comfort, or the possessing spirit's discomfort—substances to eat or drink, the first medical prescriptions were given. It was by rationalizing these prescriptions and by the tendency to use more and more only drugs that had a beneficial effect upon the patient, that therapeutics began. As the doses became more efficient, so naturally faith in the supremacy of the oral rite tended to decline and a type of magician was demanded that could specialize in the treatment of sickness by efficient manual rites—such were the first doctors.

Attention has already been called to the fact that both death and injury caused by wounds, that is to say inflicted by living mortals, are regarded by primitive peoples in quite a different light from death or injury arising out of sickness. This same distinction is manifest in the Egyptian medical papyri

73

where wounds are found to be dealt with by rational methods, and not left to the mercy of the magician and his incantations and spells. The Edwin Smith Papyrus, to which reference will be made in greater detail later on, describes the treatment of wounds, but it also contains glosses or comments upon the nature of the wound and the organs affected by them, and consequently to this document must be accorded the honour of being the earliest known scientific book. It differs entirely from the other so-called medical papyri, which do not, except in rare instances, deal with diagnosis or symptoms, and it discusses these features in a manner that shows that its compiler was attempting to record and classify systematic observations on the anatomy and physiology of the human body.

To summarize in a few words the beginnings of medical science, it may be said that disease or injury by Act of God (including spirits and demons) were regarded as supernatural and treated by magical means, whilst injuries inflicted by man were regarded rationally and treated accordingly. In other words, medicine began in the attempt to repair injuries and suffering of divine origin, and surgery in the attempt to repair the ravages of man. These points will become clearer in the next chapter in which will be discussed in more detail the nature and extent of medical knowledge in ancient Egypt. In the meantime we must glance over the documents from which our knowledge of it is derived.

These earliest medical books are a series of manuscripts written in the cursive form of hieroglyphic writing usually called *hieratic*, and are as follows.

I. Earlier Documents

(i) *The Ebers Papyrus* is the longest and most famous of these documents. It was found in a tomb at Thebes together with another medical text, the Edwin Smith Papyrus, about 1862, and was acquired by the Egyptologist whose name it bears.[1] It is now preserved in the University of Leipsic, and is in almost perfect condition. The contents are medical and magical throughout, except that on the back of the manuscript is written a calendar which has been of the utmost importance in studying the difficult and complicated problems of Egyptian chronology. The Ebers Papyrus was written about 1500 B.C., but there is abundant evidence on philological and other grounds that it was copied from a series of books many centuries older. It is stated in the papyrus itself that one passage dates from the First Dynasty (*circa* 3400 B.C.), and another extract is associated with a queen of the Sixth Dynasty. Such statements as these are of no positive value in dating, because it was in Egypt, as elsewhere, a common literary artifice to ascribe to books a very ancient origin in order to enhance their value and authority.

[1] A sumptuous facsimile in two folio volumes, with an introduction and glossary by Ludwig Stern, was published by Georg Ebers in 1875 under the title *Papyros Ebers: das Hermetische Buch über die Argnemittel der Alten Ægypter in Hieratischer Schrift*. More recently a hieroglyphic transcript of the text was issued by Dr. Walter Wreszinski : *Der Papyrus Ebers* (Leipsic 1913) [forming Vol. iii of the series of medical texts by the same editor, *Die Medezin der Alten Ägypter*]. There was a very unsatisfactory German translation by H. Joachim published many years ago.

Fortunately, however, there is no need to rely on such statements for dating Egyptian documents. Our knowledge of the writing, grammar and palæography of the papyri enables us to place them fairly accurately. Probably the books from which the Ebers Papyrus contains excerpts were written during the Twelfth and Thirteenth Dynasties, although it is likely that their subject-matter is many centuries older.

The Ebers Papyrus is not a book in the proper sense of the word : it is a miscellaneous collection of extracts and jottings collected from at least forty different sources. To call it, as Ebers did in his publication, a Hermetic Book, is entirely to mistake its nature and purpose. It consists mainly of a large collection of prescriptions for a number of named ailments, specifying the names of the drugs, the quantities of each, and the method of administration. A few sections deal with diagnosis and symptoms, another passage is physiological in character and describes the action of the heart and its vessels, and the concluding portion is surgical, being concerned with the treatment of wounds and suppurating sores. Freely interspersed amongst these elements are spells and incantations. The text covers 110 large columns (each of 22 lines on the average) in the original roll, which a modern editor has conveniently divided into 877 numbered sections of varying length. Some account of its contents will be given in the next chapter.

(ii) *The Hearst Papyrus* was discovered in 1899 by a native near Deir el-Ballas in Upper Egypt. When found, the papyrus was rolled up in an earthenware jar. In 1901 the finder brought it tied up in a head-cloth to Dr. G. Reisner, who was then excavating in the district. By him it was acquired for the University of California, where it is now preserved.[1] Owing to its having been tied up in the finder's head-cloth, the roll has been damaged in its outermost folds, and three columns of writing have thus been reduced to fragments. Otherwise, however, it is in good condition and fifteen columns (average 17 lines each) have survived almost undamaged. It contains 260 sections or prescriptions. Eight incantations are interspersed amongst the prescriptions.

The Hearst Papyrus was written somewhat later than the Ebers manuscript, for on palæographical grounds it must probably be assigned to the time of Tuthmosis III (Eighteenth Dynasty, *circa* 1501–1447 B.C.). Its contents are very similar, and in some cases at least the prescriptions are derived from the same archetypes, for many passages in the Hearst Papyrus are duplicates of some of those in the Ebers Papyrus.

(iii) *The Berlin Medical Papyrus* (Berlin Museum, No. 3038) was obtained early in the nineteenth century by the explorer Passalacqua from a tomb at

---

[1] A fine photographic facsimile of the document, with an introduction and glossary, was published by Dr. Reisner in 1905. He called the papyrus after Mrs. Phœbe Hearst, at whose expense the excavations of the University of California were carried out. *The Hearst Medical Papyrus* [University of California Publications : Egyptian Archæology, Vol. 1] (Leipsic 1905). A hieroglyphic transcript of the text was published by Wreszinski in Vol. ii of his *Die Medezin der Alten Ägypter* (Leipsic 1912).

Sakkara.[1] It dates from the reign of Rameses II
(Nineteenth Dynasty, *circa* 1292–1225 B.C.), but like
the Ebers and Hearst papyri it is derived from more
ancient sources. The manuscript is 5·16 metres in
length, and contains twenty-one columns (average
eleven lines each) on the *recto* and three columns on
the *verso*. It is the work of an indifferent scribe and
is full of corruptions and blunders. It is similar in
character to the two preceding documents and contains 204 sections. Amongst these is a duplicate of
a long passage in the Ebers Papyrus dealing with the
heart and its vessels. The pages written on the back
of the roll deal with methods of ascertaining pregnancy
and the sex of unborn children.

(iv) *The London Medical Papyrus* (British Museum,
No. 10,059) was acquired by the British Museum in
1860, from the Royal Institution, London, but nothing
appears to be known of its previous history.[2] The
manuscript is a badly-written palimpsest, dating from
the Nineteenth Dynasty, and is in fragmentary condition. It was at first thought to date from the

---

[1] A not very satisfactory lithographic facsimile of the text
was published in 1863 by Heinrich Brugsch in the second
volume of his *Recueil de Monuments Egyptiens*, Pls. 85–107.
A photographic facsimile of the document, together with a
hieroglyphic transcript, commentary and glossary was published by Dr. W. Wreszinski as Vol. i of his *Die Medezin der
Alten Agypter*, under the title *Der Grosse Medezinische Papyrus
des Berliner Museums* (Leipsic 1909).

[2] Published by Wreszinski in Vol. ii of his *Medezin* under
the title *Die Londoner Medezinische Papyrus und der Papyrus
Hearst* (Leipsic 1912). This edition has a photographic
reproduction of the original, a hieroglyphic transcription,
commentary and index of words.

Fourth Dynasty, because one of the spells mentions the name of Cheops, the builder of the Great Pyramid, but on philological and palæographical grounds, it cannot be older than the time of Rameses II, although like the other documents, its subject-matter is of far earlier origin. It contains fewer prescriptions and a greater number of incantations than the other medical papyri and bears a greater resemblance to the magical papyri of Leiden than to the Ebers or Hearst papyri. Its text has been divided into sixty-three sections, eleven of which are duplicated in the Ebers Papyrus, but the last three of the nineteen surviving columns are too fragmentary to allow of their contents being divided into sections and numbered.

(v) *The Kahun Medical Papyrus* was discovered amongst a large mass of papyrus fragments by Sir Flinders Petrie at Illahun when excavating in 1889 in the Faŷum, in Lower Egypt.[1] It is older in date than any of the other medical documents, and must be assigned to the Twelfth or Thirteenth Dynasties, probably to the reign of Amenemmes III (*circa* 1850 B.C.). The innumerable fragments of which it consists were sorted and pieced together with great skill by Prof. F. Ll. Griffith, who found that they make up the greater part of three columns of a roll whose beginning and end are both lost. Although in fragmentary condition the greater part of its contents is legible, and they consist of thirty-four sections (including one incantation), all dealing with one subject —gynæcology. The sections in this papyrus do not

[1] Published by F. Ll. Griffith, *Hieratic Papyri from Kahun and Gurob* (London 1898), Text vol., pp. 5–11, Plates vol., Pls. 5 and 6.

consist, like most of those of the other papyri, of prescriptions, but of *directions* for the treatment of various vaginal and uterine disorders. There is also a portion that deals with pregnancy and sex-determination, as in the Berlin Medical Papyrus.

(vi) *Berlin Papyrus, No. 3027.* This document was acquired by the Berlin Museum in 1886 from an English lady, Miss Westcar, at the same time as the famous papyrus that bears her name, and that deals with the wonder-working magicians of the Pyramid Age.[1] It was first published by Dr. Adolf Erman in 1901 [2] in transcription with a translation and commentary. The whole of the hieratic text was published some years later in an official publication of the Berlin Museum.[3] The document is often referred to in Egyptological literature as *Mutter und Kind.* This papyrus was written in the Eighteenth Dynasty about the middle of the fifteenth century before Christ, but is a copy of an older original. It consists of nine pages on the *recto* and six on the *verso* containing altogether about twenty incantations, with some prescriptions interspersed, for the protection of mothers and new-born babies from the dangers of possession by hostile spirits and for the cure of infantile ailments. Of especial medical interest are the two long lists of parts of the body and internal organs that occur in one of the incantations.

[1] See above, p. 53.

[2] *Abhandlungen der Königl. Preuss. Akademie der Wissenschaften zu Berlin*, 1901, under the title *Zaubersprüche für Mutter und Kind*, 52 pp. and 2 plates.

[3] *Hieratische Papyrus aus den Koeniglichen Museum zu Berlin* (1911), Band III, taf. 17–25.

(vii) *The Edwin Smith Papyrus* was found at Thebes together with the Ebers Papyrus in 1862. It remained in the possession of the late Mr. Edwin Smith until his death in 1906, when it passed to his daughter, Miss Leonora Smith, who presented it to the New York Historical Society, in the library of which institution it is now preserved. The document has been exhaustively studied by Prof. James Henry Breasted of Chicago, and he is about to publish a full edition of it. In the meantime our information respecting this, the most important of all the medical papyri, is contained in three preliminary accounts of the manuscript that Prof. Breasted published in 1922.[1] The Edwin Smith Papyrus deals with forty-eight cases of wounds and their treatment, and on the back of the document are extracts from two magical books. It is a little earlier in date than the Ebers Papyrus.

(viii) *Other Documents.* A fragment of a veterinary papyrus dealing with diseases of animals was discovered amongst the papyri of Illahun.[2] This document is too short to justify any opinion on Egyptian veterinary medicine, but its existence alone is of great interest as showing that books on this subject were drawn up as early as the Middle Kingdom.

[1] *New York Historical Society, Quarterly Bulletin*, Vol. vi (April 1922), pp. 4–31 ; *Bulletin of the Society of Medical History of Chicago*, Vol. iii (January 1923), pp. 385–429; *Recueil d'Etudes Egyptologiques dédiées à la Mémoire de Jean-François Champollion* (Paris 1922), pp. 385–429.

[2] F. Ll. Griffith, *Hieratic Papyri from Kahun and Gurob* (London 1898), Text vol., pp. 12–14, Plates vol., Pl. vii.

The Westcar Papyrus, to which reference was made in Chapter IV, is not a medical document, but a series of popular stories on the feats worked by magicians in the Pyramid Age. It contains one passage, however, of great medical interest: this is a graphic description of the birth of triplets and it throws much light on ancient Egyptian methods of accouchement.[1]

In the Leiden Museum there is an interesting series of Magical Papyri, which although containing principally incantations and charms, are medical in so far as their purpose is the prevention and cure of disease. Some medical prescriptions are interspersed amongst this magical matter. There are incantations for the cure of an unidentified disease called *smewni*, remedies for headaches, burns, scorpion-stings, poison, etc., and there is 'a book for repelling fear'.[2] These papyri, as a whole, have not yet been edited, but many years ago a lithographic facsimile of the hieratic texts was published.[3]

A large number of magical papyri is included in the fine series of hieratic documents of the Nineteenth and Twentieth Dynasties now preserved in the Museum of Turin. Most of these are collections of spells and incantations against possessing spirits, disease, snakes, scorpions, etc. One passage enumer-

---

[1] *Westcar Papyrus*, 9, 21–11, 18; G. Maspero, *Popular Stories of Ancient Egypt* (London 1915), pp. 36–40; A. Erman, *The Literature of the Ancient Egyptians* [transl. by A. M. Blackman], (London 1927), pp. 44–46.

[2] *Leiden Papyri*, I. 343 + 345, 347, 348, 349.

[3] C. Leemans, *Ægyptische Monumenten van het Nederlandsche Museum van Oudheden te Leyden.*

ates all the possible ways in which death may befall a man.[1]

In the Vatican Library there is a magical papyrus of the Twentieth Dynasty that contains a list of organs of the body,[2] and in the Louvre Museum is a limestone ostracon inscribed with four prescriptions for the ear.[3]

The miscellaneous character of the contents of the medical papyri (i–iv) mentioned above, suggests that they are copies, made for the use of general practitioners who lived in places where the libraries of the temples were not easily accessible to them. According to Herodotus,[4] all the physicians of Egypt were specialists, and this statement may have in it an element of truth, for although the medical papyri that have come down to us are clearly intended for the use of practitioners who had to be prepared to deal with cases of every possible kind, the fact is nevertheless clear that they are made up of excerpts from a number of separate books each dealing with an individual branch of medicine, and this fact presupposes that each of the prototypes was the work of a specialist.

II. LATER DOCUMENTS

In addition to the papyri already enumerated, most of which date from the New Kingdom (Dynasties

[1] The Turin magical papyri, like those of Leiden, have not yet been fully edited. Facsimiles of the hieratic texts are published in W. Pleyte and F. Rossi, *Papyrus de Turin* (Leiden 1869–1876).

[2] *Vatican Papyrus, No.* 36. See A. Erman, *Zeitschrift für äg. Sprache*, Bd. 31 (1893), pp. 119 ff.

[3] *Louvre Ostracon, No.* 3255.   [4] Book ii, cap. 84.

7

XVIII to XX) it may be mentioned that there are medical and magical books known that belong to much later periods. Of these the most famous is the manuscript part of which is now in the British Museum and part in Leiden, generally known as the *London-Leiden Magical Papyrus*.[1] This document was written in the third century of the Christian Era, and its contents show that the belief in magic was then as strong as it had been many centuries earlier. A large part of this papyrus is devoted to divination and erotic charms, but a considerable proportion of it deals with spells and prescriptions for the prevention and cure of disease.

Reference must also be made to the Coptic medical documents. The principal of these is a long papyrus found in 1892 at Meshaîkh, near the site of the ancient Lepidotonpolis, and it is now in the French Archæological Institute at Cairo.[2] This manuscript must be assigned to the ninth or tenth century A.D., and is written in Coptic, the language of the Christian Egyptians. It is purged of magic, but its arrangement and contents betray its ancient origin, for its

---

[1] Published *in extenso* by Prof. F. Ll. Griffith and Sir Herbert Thompson in three volumes. *The Demotic Magical Papyrus of London and Leiden* (London 1904–1909). Vol. i (8vo) contains introduction and translation, Vol. ii (folio) facsimile of the demotic text; Vol. iii (4to) glossary and indices.

[2] Published *in extenso* with facsimile, translation, introduction and indices by E. Chassinat, *Un Papyrus Médical Copte* (Cairo 1921) [*Mémoires* of the French Institute, t. xxxii]. I published an account of this papyrus and its contents in the *Proceedings of the Royal Society of Medicine*, Vol. xvii (1924), pp. 51–56.

general make-up is very similar to that of the medical books compiled in the time of the Pharaohs. The ground-work is identical, and it only differs in the fact that many drugs of Greek and Arabic origin had been added to the pharmacopœia. Spells and incantations are entirely absent from this document (although they occur in other Coptic writings), and the patient has generally to rely on the treatment prescribed by the physician without magical or divine aid : to a very few prescriptions the words are added ' he will be cursed if it please God ', or ' he will recover by the power of God '. The author was discriminating in the choice of the prescriptions he wrote down from the various traditional sources from which he must have gathered them. One or two of them appear to be original ; for instance, one of his remedies he calls ' a great remedy on which I have worked myself, with my father ', and of another he says, ' a good collyrium on which I have worked with my father ; great is its virtue '. There is one prescription, a comprehensive remedy for diseases of the spleen, for a crooked body or limbs, for calculi, and also an emmenagogue, and of this the author says it is a remedy ' which we found written in the books of the ancients '. This Coptic papyrus is a collection of recipes only (237 in number), and it provides no information as to diagnosis (which is always assumed) nor any clinical or surgical directions. Some of the prescriptions show Greek influence, especially one for ' black bile ' (No. 70), which is evidently influenced by Avicenna, Dioscorides and Alexander of Tralles, but the author did not slavishly copy any of these writings, although he must have been familiar with them. That the author was a physician and the son of a physician is evident from the passages quoted above, and also from such remarks as these: 'we have experimented with this remedy and found it perfect' (No. 109), 'I have experimented with this powder and found it perfect, it is without equal in efficacy' (No. 80).

Before leaving the subject of Coptic medicine, it may be mentioned that in addition to this manuscript, some smaller Coptic medical fragments are known. In the Vatican are two leaves of parchment that once formed part of a book, and these contain forty-five prescriptions.[1] Another fragment, also a leaf from a book, was discovered in 1887 at Deir el-Abiad ('The White Monastery'). This contains eleven prescriptions for affections of the breasts.[2] The remainder of the material consists of a number of small fragments, now dispersed amongst several collections, the British Museum,[3] the John Rylands Library, Manchester,[4] and the Berlin Museum.[5] In addition to these medical documents, there exist certain Coptic magical

[1] G. Zoëga, *Catalogus Codicum Copticorum* (Rome 1810), pp. 626–630.

[2] Urbain Bouriant, 'Fragment d'un Livre de Médécine en Copte Thébain,' *Comptes Rendus de l'Acad. des Inscriptions et Belles-lettres*, t. xv (1887), pp. 374–378.

[3] W. E. Crum, *Catalogue of Coptic Manuscripts in the British Museum* (London 1905), pp. 255–256.

[4] W. E. Crum, *Catalogue of Coptic Manuscripts in the John Rylands Library* (Manchester 1909), pp. 52–60; H. R. Hall, *Coptic and Greek Texts of the Christian Period* (London 1905), pp. 64–66.

[5] *Koptische Urkunden aus den Kgl. Museum zu Berlin* (Berlin 1904), Bd. i, taf. 24, 25, 29.

texts, some of which are concerned with the treatment or cure of disease.

A number of Egyptian medical papyri written in Greek has been recovered from the sites of various Greek settlements in Egypt. Most of them hail from Oxyrhynchus, that mine of literary discovery.[1]

All the medical papyri of Egypt are anonymous : there are no names in Egypt to compare with those of Hippocrates, Galen or Dioscorides in Greece. The names of several famous magicians, sages or physicians who lived in the time of the Pharaohs have come down to us—Imhotep,[2] Amenophis the son of Hapu [3] and others—but it is not known that they wrote medical books. It is possible that they composed learned works, but if so, these books have been sunk in the ocean of Time.

[1] B. P. Grenfell and A. S. Hunt, *The Oxyrhynchus Papyri*, Pt. ii (London 1899), p. 134, No. 234 ; A. S. Hunt, *ibid.*, Pt. viii (1911), p. 110, No. 1088 ; Grenfell, Hunt and Goodspeed, *The Tebtunis Papyri*, Pt. ii (1902), p. 20, No. 272 ; p. 22, No. 273 ; A. S. Hunt, *Catalogue of Greek Papyri in the John Rylands Library*, Vol. i, pp. 55 ff., Nos. 28, 29, 29B ; B. P. Grenfell, *An Alexandrian Erotic Fragment and Other Greek Papyri* (Oxford 1896), p. 85, No. I, 52 ; A. Bäckström, *Archiv für Papyrusforschung*, Bd. iii (1906), pp. 157–162 (Golenischeff Papyrus), etc.

[2] Imhotep became posthumously a medical demi-god and in Ptolemaic times he was promoted to the full rank of a divinity ; he was identified by the Greeks with Asklepios. For a full account of this remarkable personage, see the monograph *Imhotep*, 2nd edn. (Oxford 1928), by Dr. J. B. Hurry.

[3] I have summarized all that is known of this sage, who also was deified in Ptolemaic times, in ' Amenophis the Son of Hapu ', *Ægyptus*, Vol. vii (Milan 1926), pp. 113–138.

CHAPTER VI

ANCIENT EGYPTIAN MEDICINE

THE contents of the papyri enumerated in the last chapter, although they abound in difficulties, enable us to form a pretty clear idea of the nature and extent of the medical knowledge of the Egyptians. As regards Anatomy and Physiology, attention has already been called to the important part played by the custom of mummification in the history of anatomy and medicine. The complex manipulations to which the body of an Egyptian was subjected during the process of embalming, that have been described in Chapter III, for many centuries afforded opportunities for its practitioners to become familiar with the appearance, nature and mutual positions of the internal organs of the body, opportunities that were denied to all peoples who cremated or inhumed their dead.

The most important influence, however, of the custom of mummification upon the history of medicine was the fact that it familiarized the popular mind for over twenty centuries with the idea of cutting the dead human body. Thus ' Egypt made it possible for the Greek physicians of the Ptolemaic age to begin, for the first time, the systematic dissection of the human body, which popular prejudice forbade in all other parts of the world'. [1]

Mummification, involving as it did, the removal and handling of the viscera, had an enormous influence on the growth of science, for it provided for the first time opportunities for observations on Comparative Anatomy. In the course of embalming a body, most of the internal organs, both abdominal and thoracic, were removed, with the exception of the heart, which was almost always carefully left *in situ*, attached to its great vessels. These organs, when severed from their connections, were separately washed and embalmed, and for many centuries it was customary to make them up into four parcels and to place them into four special vases, usually known as Canopic Jars, each of which was under the protection of one of the Four Children of Horus, and from the Nineteenth Dynasty onwards, the stoppers of these jars were fashioned in the form of the heads of these four divinities, one being human, and the other three those of a falcon, a jackal and a baboon respectively. During the Twenty-first Dynasty the use of these ceremonial jars fell into abeyance, and the organs were wrapped in linen packages together with wax models of their appropriate guardian deities, and the parcels were replaced within the vacant body-cavity. The special treatment of the viscera familiarized the Egyptians, as has been noted, with the appearance and mutual positions of the organs, and this familiarity with them enabled them to recognize the analogies between the viscera of the human body and those of

[1] G. Elliot Smith, *Journal of Egyptian Archæology*, Vol. i (1914), p. 190.

animals, the latter long familiar from the time-honoured custom of cutting-up animals for sacrifice and for food. It is a noteworthy fact that the various hieroglyphic signs representing parts of the body, and especially the internal organs, are pictures of the organs of mammals and not of human beings. This shows that the Egyptians' knowledge of the internal structure of animals is older than their knowledge of that of man : it shows further that they recognized the essential identity of the two, for they borrowed the signs based on the organs of animals and used them unaltered when speaking of the corresponding organs of the human body.[1] Thus the hieroglyph for 'heart' is the heart of an ox, not that of a man,[2] and the word for 'throat' or 'gullet' is determined with the head and wind-pipe of an ox.[3] The word for 'womb' is the bicornate uterus of a cow[4]; for 'ear' a mammalian ear[5]; for 'tooth' an animal's tusk[6]; for 'tongue' an animal's tongue.[7] The signs representing the ribs, backbone, intestines and others, are similarly borrowed from mammalian anatomy.[8] There are other hieroglyphic signs, whose original meanings are lost, that are borrowed from mammalian anatomy : the sign *nfr* (heart and wind-pipe), *sm'* (lung and wind-pipe) and *ht* (teats and tail),[9]

---

[1] From which it follows that the custom of mummification, old as it was, was of *relatively* late growth.

[2] For a complete list of hieroglyphs based on parts of mammals, see A. H. Gardiner, *Egyptian Grammar* (Oxford 1927), pp. 453–458, Nos. F. 1–F. 52. The 'heart' sign is No. 34.

[3] F. 10.   [4] F. 45.   [5] F. 21.   [6] F. 18.   [7] F. 20.

[8] F. 42, F. 43 ; F. 39, F. 40, F. 41 ; F. 46–49, etc.

[9] F. 35 ; F. 36 ; F. 32.

although not employed as anatomical terms, were anatomical in origin.   The hieroglyphs denoting external parts of the body are mostly borrowed from human anatomy.

The extent of the knowledge of a people in respect of any given technical subject can be gauged to some extent by the richness or otherwise of its terminology. In the ancient Egyptian language, there are over one hundred anatomical terms, and this fact alone shows that the Egyptians were able to differentiate and name a great many organs and parts of the body that a more primitive and less enlightened people would have grouped together or failed to perceive.   Whilst, however, the Egyptians' terminology for the gross anatomy of the body is fairly accurate, they entirely failed to understand the nerves, muscles, arteries and veins.   They had but one word to denote all these structures : they appear to have regarded them all as various parts of a single system of branching and radiating channels forming a network over all parts of the body.   The word that is used for the blood-vessels communicating with the heart is the same as that employed for the muscles in the prescriptions for stiff joints and rheumatoid complaints.   In such cases it is only from the context that we can gather exactly what is meant.

As regards physiology, the most important document that has survived is a long passage in the Ebers Papyrus that deals with the heart and its ' vessels '.[1]

---

[1] *Ebers Papyrus*, 99, 1–103, 18 ; *Berlin Medical Papyrus*, 15, 1–17, 1. Prof. Breasted states that a fragmentary passage in the Edwin Smith Papyrus shows that that document also once contained a further duplicate of this text.

The passage is obscure, corrupt, and very difficult to understand, and the duplicate of it in the Berlin Medical Papyrus is so faulty and so incorrectly written that it affords us little help. The Egyptians themselves, indeed, must have felt the difficulty of understanding the passage, for many glosses were introduced in ancient times with the object of explaining the meaning of the sentences. These glosses may have helped the Egyptians of the Eighteenth Dynasty, but to us of to-day they afford but little assistance. The passage is an extract from another book, as we learn from its heading. It begins thus:

'The beginning of the Science of the Physician: to know the movement of the heart and to know the heart. There are vessels attached to it for every member.' An explanatory gloss follows: 'As to this: if any physician, any priest or any magician place his hands or his fingers upon the head, upon the occiput, upon the hands, upon the site of the heart, upon the arms, upon the legs, he will make examination for the heart on account of its vessels for every member.' The meaning of this obscurely worded gloss is plain enough: the pulse can be felt in various parts of the body as well as in the region of the heart itself because of the vessels that radiate over the body from that centre. There is, of course, no hint in this passage of any knowledge of the circulation of the blood (although some writers have read this meaning into the text), nor in fact is there any mention at all of blood: all that was perceived was the sympathy of the pulse with the beating of the heart itself. The Egyptians certainly regarded the heart as the most important organ of the body.

It was held to be the seat of intelligence and of all
the emotions (they apparently attached no importance
at all to the brain), and its presence in the body was
so essential to existence, that it was not removed
from the body during the process of embalming, but
was carefully left, attached to the great vessels, in
its place in the thorax although all the surrounding
viscera were cut away.

The text, after this introductory paragraph, proceeds
to enumerate the vessels that communicate with each
part of the body, and their functions. 'There are
four vessels from his [1] nostrils, of which 2 give mucus
and 2 give blood.' Similarly there are four vessels
from the inside of the temples that supply blood to
the back of the eyes. A gloss explains that tears
are created by the lids, and not supplied by vessels.
There are four vessels distributed over the head of
which the hinder ones supply nutriment to the hair.
It is next stated that air enters the nostrils, and thence
passes to the heart and lungs. What follows is very
obscure, but it apparently describes the behaviour of
the heart when it receives an excess of fluid. 'There
are four vessels for his two ears, two on his left side
and two on his right side : the breath of life enters
by his right ear and the breath of death enters by his
left ear.' [2] There are three vessels for each arm and
each leg, two for the testicles which supply them with

---

[1] The medical texts never speak in the abstract of *the*
heart, *the* nostrils, etc. There is always a hypothetical patient
implied whose case is being discussed.

[2] *Ebers*, 100, 1–5. The concept of death entering the left
ear explains a prescription in the *Berlin Medical Papyrus*,
6, 10, bearing the title ' To frighten death from the ear'.

semen, and four for the liver, supplying air and moisture. There are four vessels for the lungs and for the spleen, these also are stated to convey air and water. There are two vessels for the penis which supply urine, and four for the anus, which is said to communicate with the vessels on the sides of the body and those supplying the limbs. The text continues with a description of the behaviour of the heart under various conditions, and with a further reference to the vessels in various parts of the body.

Nothing like a system of physiology can be reconstructed from this obscure and garbled passage, although one or two facts emerge quite clearly. One is the importance of the heart in the vascular system, and the other is the belief that the ' vessels ' were not exclusively concerned with blood, but were the vehicles also of air, water, semen, and other secretions. This erroneous conclusion probably arose out of the conditions observed during the post-mortem manipulations of the embalmers. It will also be observed that the ears, besides being the organs of hearing, were thought to be part of the pulmonary system, for it is stated that the breaths of life and of death enter them. Beneath all this jumble of statement that fills several pages of the papyrus, much of which is erroneous, there remains a nucleus of correctly observed truth, which shows that in very early times a serious attempt was being made to understand the structure and the functions of the body and its organs.

Reference has been made to the importance attached to the heart, and in this connection attention may be directed to the well-known picture, so common in funerary papyri and on mummy-cases, that represents the weighing of the heart in the balance, in which it counterpoises the emblem of truth. Religious texts frequently refer to the heart and to its necessity to the welfare both of the living and the dead. It is affirmed of a dead man for his welfare that 'his own true heart is with him', and the *Book of the Dead* is full of spells to safeguard the heart and to prevent its destruction by hostile powers. All these texts show clearly the belief that the individual could not do without his heart either as a living man or a mummy.

There is a long passage in the Ebers Papyrus that is an extract from a book dealing with disorders of the stomach. It may be noted in passing that the Egyptian word for stomach is literally 'mouth of the heart', and it is interesting to compare the Greek words στόμαχος and στόμα. The cases in this book are quite differently arranged from the other remedies in the papyrus, for they describe the symptoms and diagnosis as well as the treatment. In nearly all the other medical books the diagnosis is assumed.[1] This collection of cases is labelled 'Directions for illness of the Stomach'.[2] There are twenty different affections of the stomach described in this passage, and they are drawn up on one model. The opening words are 'If you examine a man who suffers in the stomach', then follows a description of the symptoms, after which is the formula, 'You say concerning it: "It is so and so" (diagnosis). Then comes the treat-

[1] There are some few diagnosed cases interspersed amongst the remedies, e.g. *Ebers*, 51, 19–52, 7. The Ebers Papyrus has altogether 47 diagnosed cases.

[2] *Ebers Papyrus*, 36, 4–43, 2.

ment : "You do for it so and so." ' A prescription of drugs then follows, with directions as to their administration, i.e. the quantity, how often to be taken, whether at night or morning, before or after food, etc. There are sometimes added observations on the state of the fæces and other particulars. This collection of cases marks a great advance in real scientific observation and treatment.

In considering the pathology of the papyri, the student is at once confronted with a host of difficulties. In the first place, the texts are full of philological and lexicographical problems, and they are written in a specialized, concise and aphoristic style abounding in syntactical difficulties. Many of the passages, as already noted, have been copied from older books and show evidence of textual corruption. But the greatest difficulty of all is the impossibility of translating into English the names of a great number of the maladies mentioned, and the names of most of the drugs. There are, for instance, some half-dozen words for which no closer equivalent can be found than ' swelling ' or ' lump ', although each of the many terms clearly conveyed a specific meaning to the Egyptians : in such cases the translator is obliged to rely on the context alone, which is not always very enlightening. Some of these ' swellings ' are clearly boils and carbuncles of various kinds, suppurating or otherwise, but others again are to my mind unmistakably manifestations of bilharzia infection, which was in ancient times, as it is to-day, a terrible menace to the inhabitants of the Nile Valley.[1]

[1] In this connection see F. C. Madden, *The Surgery of Egypt* (Cairo 1919).

Generally speaking, the maladies with which the ancient papyri are concerned are those which attack the *fellaḥîn* of to-day. Intestinal troubles due to bad water, to worms and other parasites, ophthalmia and a very large number of other affections of the eyes, boils, carbuncles, skin diseases and the bites of insects and snakes, bilharzia infection, vaginal disorders and middle-ear disease, figure amongst the many maladies for which the ancient physician had to find remedies. The heterogeneous nature of the ailments, injuries and diseases cannot be better shown than by running rapidly through the contents of the longest of the medical documents—the Ebers Papyrus. After some introductory incantations, the papyrus commences with a long series of prescriptions for maladies of the stomach and bowels (including the use of purgatives and diuretics), for pains and swellings in the abdomen, and for getting rid of various kinds of intestinal worms. Another group deals with the prevention of vomiting and the promotion of appetite and good digestion. As might be supposed, a very long section is devoted to diseases of the eyes, a quite natural state of affairs in a country where eye troubles abound. There are also prescriptions for the lungs, liver and stomach (the latter, as mentioned above, very elaborate, with symptoms, diagnosis and treatment). Next follows a series of remedies for the head and scalp, including such complaints as alopecia, and ointments to prevent the hair from falling out or turning grey. Other sections deal with fevers, and with affections of the mouth, teeth, tongue, throat and ears, among the latter being one for ' an ear that emits a foul discharge '. A long series of remedies is provided for 'relaxing stiffness of the muscles', for 'easing the muscles', or for 'easing stiff joints'—clearly rheumatoid complaints:[1] then follows a section devoted to diseases of women, and this is followed in turn by a collection of household recipes, such as ridding the house of fleas, mice, snakes and other vermin. Between these useful hints and the concluding section, which deals with boils and suppurating sores, is inserted the treatise on the heart and its vessels to which reference has already been made.

Taken as a whole, the Ebers Papyrus contains, besides incantations, about forty groups of remedies and prescriptions that can be differentiated, and out of its total number of 877 sections, there are only forty-seven diagnosed cases: in the great majority of remedies the diagnosis is taken for granted.

The earliest form of surgery known (other than the manipulations of mummification) is the rite of circumcision, but this must be eliminated entirely from the domain of medicine, as it was a religious observance.[2] Until recently, all we knew of Egyptian surgery was derived from the concluding portion of the Ebers Papyrus, but the publication of the Edwin Smith Papyrus provides us with a mass of new information.

[1] Rheumatoid arthritis was extremely common in ancient Egypt, and many skeletons have been found revealing clear evidence of its effects. The papyri indicate that the 'stiffness' was seated in the limbs, the joints, the spine and the pelvis.

[2] On the walls of a Sixth Dynasty tomb at Sakkara there is a bas-relief in which this operation is depicted. See J. Capart, *Une Rue de Tombeaux* (Brussels 1907), Pl. 66.

It has already been indicated that the Edwin Smith Papyrus differs from all other medical papyri (except the latter part of the Ebers Papyrus and the Kahun Papyrus) in that it is not a mere collection of prescriptions but a handbook of practical treatment applied to wounds. It deals, therefore, not with remedies but with cases. The cases are wounds in various parts of the body, starting at the top of the head and proceeding downwards as far as the thorax. The text comes to an abrupt end at this point, and in its present state it contains forty-eight cases, but the entire work from which it was copied presumably completed the exploration of the body down to the feet. This 'head to foot' method of arranging the materials may be claimed as evidence in favour of the scientific and systematic character of the book; but it is, after all, a very natural sequence. The same order is followed in the numerous lists of the parts of the body to which reference was made in Chapter IV (some of these lists terminate with the words 'there is no part of his body without its god from the top of his head to the soles of his feet') and it was a common arrangement in Greek medical books. The surgical text of the Edwin Smith Papyrus breaks off when it reaches the breast, and the scribe resumed his labours by copying extracts from two other works, both magical: the one, 'Incantations for driving out the wind in the year of pest', and the other, 'The Book for transforming an old man into a youth of twenty'. [1]

[1] The quest of a means of securing perpetual youth has occupied the thoughts of man from very early times. The Edwin Smith Papyrus gives us the prescription for the earliest

8

The cases are presented in a systematic fashion, and they all contain the following elements : Title, Examination, Diagnosis, Verdict, Treatment. In many cases glosses are added that afford additional information as to the exact meaning of the terms and idioms of the text. The treatment is throughout appropriate and rational, and in this respect it conforms to the principle already mentioned, namely that rational methods are to be expected when wounds inflicted by human agency are being dealt with. Professor Breasted claims that the discovery of this papyrus destroys the opinion generally held that Egyptian medicine originated in magic. He believes that this document affords evidence that anatomy was practised for its own sake, and that therefore the Edwin Smith Papyrus is in the true sense a scientific book. Whilst fully agreeing with the latter opinion, it seems to me that too much is claimed for this single manuscript, on the very back of which two magical texts are written. It does not in the least detract from the value and importance of the document to prefer the opinion that while it undoubtedly affords evidence that a serious attempt was being made to understand anatomy, it must be clearly borne in mind that it deals only with injuries or wounds, and not with diseases, for which perforce magical methods had to

known quack-medicine claiming to achieve this result, and it is interesting to compare with it the following extract from a leaflet issued by a London quack in 1680. He claims for his ' Great Restorer ' that ' it has that miraculous operation that renders old men and women of three or four score as youthful as those of twenty or thirty years of age ' (C. J. S. Thompson, *The Quacks of Old London* (London 1928), p. 199 ; cf. also pp. 248 ff.).

be employed because the cause of disease was to the ancients invisible, impalpable and unknown.

In the Ebers Papyrus, as already mentioned, there is a section devoted to surgical cases.[1] These are similar in arrangement to the cases in the Edwin Smith Papyrus, and sometimes contain an expression found in the 'verdicts' of the latter : 'it is an ailment it will contend with', i.e. a curable malady.[2] These cases appear to be boils or tumours, and directions are given for diagnosing them, and for lancing and dissecting them. Instructions are given for locating the trouble, for incising the swelling, for fastening back the edges of the wound, for removing the morbid contents, and for cleansing and dressing it. Surgical instruments have been discovered in Egypt, amongst which are delicate scalpels, probes, forceps and knives. For fractured limbs, splints were used.[3] In spite of oft-repeated statements to the contrary, there is no evidence whatever that tooth-stopping, or any other form of dental surgery, was practised by the Egyptians in Pharaonic times.

There are three forms of 'verdict' in the Edwin Smith Papyrus, two of which are found in other documents. They are (i) 'It is an ailment I will treat'; (ii) 'It is an ailment I will contend with'; and (iii) 'An untreatable ailment'. The first of these implies confidence in a cure, the second implies a

[1] *Ebers Papyrus*, 103, 19–110, 9.
[2] *Ebers*, 105, 12 ; cf. *Edwin Smith* cases, Nos. 4, 7, 21, 28, 29, 37, 45, 47. The expression 'contend with' seems to retain a lingering notion of dealing with possessing spirits.
[3] G. Elliot Smith, 'The Earliest Splints', *British Medical Journal*, Mar. 28, 1908.

difficult case that must be seriously grappled with, but the third is used in cases that the physician foresees to be hopeless. Thirteen out of forty-eight cases in the Edwin Smith Papyrus are so designated as beyond hope. The magician claimed omnipotence ; the physician, on the other hand, knew the limits of his powers.

Childbirth did not come within the scope of medical practice in Egypt, although some of the Papyri contain spells for facilitating delivery and assuaging the pains of labour.[1] Egyptian women in childbirth crouched on a bed or birth-stool with their legs bent under them, their bodies being in a vertical position. The midwives who assisted were usually two in number. One placed herself behind the patient and clasped her round the body during the pains of labour, thus affording a firm support, the other knelt in front ready to receive the infant. Delivery was often assisted by massage. The new-born child was washed by the midwife, who also cut the umbilical cord. The Kahun Papyrus and one section of the Ebers Papyrus deal with the diagnosis and treatment of various kinds of vaginal and uterine complaints such as prolapsus, and with menstruation. In addition to these, methods are given for ascertaining whether a woman is barren or fertile, whether conception has taken place, and with the sex of unborn children, and the use of contraceptives is also mentioned.[2]

---

[1] *Berlin Papyrus*, 3027, 5, 8–6, 8 ; *Leiden Papyrus*, I. 348, 12, 2–6.

[2] I have dealt with ancient contraceptive methods in the chapter ' Early Ideas concerning Conception and Contraception ' in the collective work, *Medical Help on Birth Control* (London 1928), pp. 189–200.

Such, in outline, is the nature and extent of medical practice in ancient Egypt. In later chapters some account will be given of the *materia medica* of the ancient Egyptians and some survivals of their practices that have persisted almost to the present day. In the meantime a few words may be said as to the actual evidence of disease afforded by Egyptian mummies and skeletons.[1]

Numerous cases of calculi have been found : stone in the bladder, as early as predynastic times, and in the kidney, in bodies of the Second Dynasty, also a single case of gall-stones in a female mummy of the Twenty-first Dynasty. Bilharzia eggs were found in the kidneys of two mummies of the Twenty-first Dynasty by the late Sir Marc Armand Ruffer.[2]

Several cases of arterial disease have been found and reported upon by the late Prof. Shattock[3] and by Sir Marc A. Ruffer.[4] During the examination of a large series of mummies of the Twenty-first Dynasty Prof. Elliot Smith found a typical case of Pott's disease with severe spinal curvature and a large psoas abscess.[5] Several cases of hip-disease have been noted.[6]

[1] These are mainly summarized from the chapter by Prof. G. Elliot Smith in Elliot Smith and Dawson, *Egyptian Mummies* (London 1924), pp. 154–162. I have added some cases that have since come to my notice.

[2] *British Medical Journal*, Jan. 1, 1910, p. 16 (the mummies are there wrongly stated to be of the Twentieth Dynasty).

[3] *Lancet*, January 30, 1909 (microscopic sections of the aorta of the Pharaoh Meneptah).

[4] *Journal of Pathology and Bacteriology*, Vol. xv (1911).

[5] K. Sudhoff's *Zur historischen Biologie der Krankheitserreger*, Heft 3, 1910. It is the mummy of Nespeheran.

[6] *Bulletin of the Archæological Survey of Nubia*, No. 3 (Cairo 1909), p. 31.

A large osteo-sarcoma of the femur and two cases of osteo-sarcoma of the head of the humerus were found in the Fifth Dynasty necropolis of Gizeh, but no evidence of true carcinoma occurs until Byzantine times, when cases of malignant disease, one involving the base of the skull and the other the sacrum, suggest the presence of squamous-celled carcinoma of the naso-pharynx and of the rectum respectively.

Two cases of talipes have been recorded. One was the Pharaoh Siptah of the Nineteenth Dynasty [1] and the other a priest of the Twelfth Dynasty.[2] A case of true gout was found in an elderly man of the early Christian period from Philæ. Large masses of white concretions were found on the metatarsal bones of the great toes, and smaller masses surrounded the metatarso-phalangeal joints of all the toes except the small ones. These concretions were held in position by the tendons passing over them. There were also concretions on the tarsal bones, the ends of the tibiæ and fibulæ, the posterior surfaces of the patellæ and the patellar ligaments. The hands and arms were affected similarly but less severely. The white concretions were found to yield the typical reactions of uric acid. This interesting specimen is now in the Museum of the Royal College of Surgeons, London.[3]

Dental caries is very rare in predynastic and

---

[1] G. Elliot Smith, *The Royal Mummies* (Cairo 1912), p. 71 and Pl. 62.

[2] M. A. Murray and others, *The Tomb of Two Brothers* (Manchester 1910), p. 42.

[3] G. Elliot Smith, *Bulletin of the Archæological Survey of Nubia* (Cairo 1908), p. 32 and Pl. 23.

protodynastic remains, and among the poorer people whose diet was mainly uncooked vegetable food it never became common. The rapid wearing-down of the teeth by coarse food opened-up the pulp-cavities, and thus created a ready seat for infection. Accordingly alveolar abscesses without dental caries are common. During and after the Pyramid Age when luxurious living was in vogue amongst the wealthier classes, dental caries, alveolar abscesses and tartar-formation are frequently encountered conditions.[1]

Rheumatoid arthritis was so extremely common in Egypt and Nubia, that it is rare, especially in earlier times, to find any adult skeleton that does not reveal its effects.[2]

Various inflammatory conditions of the bones have been found. These include chronic rhinitis,[3] mastoid disease,[4] and various forms of cranial ulceration, many of which are of great pathological interest.[5]

[1] *Archæological Survey of Nubia* : *Report for* 1907–8 (Cairo 1910), Vol. ii, *Report on the Human Remains*, by G. Elliot Smith and F. Wood-Jones, p. 281. (This volume will be hereafter cited as ' *Report* '.)

[2] *Report*, pp. 272 ff. [3] *Report*, p. 283. [4] *Report*, p 284.

[5] *Report*, p. 285. From the historical point of view the pathological conditions revealed by the skull of the Rhodesian Man, now in the British Museum (Natural History), are of very great interest. Mr. Macleod Yearsley, F.R.C.S., has contributed an interesting appendix to the official report on the fossil (W. P. Pycraft and others, *Rhodesian Man and Associated Remains*, London 1928, pp. 59–63), and the following extract is taken from his conclusions. ' The chronic septic condition of the mouth led to suppurative middle ear disease, complicated with mastoid abscess. That this abscess broke through the cortex at the base of the mastoid and tracked upwards into the temporal fossa along the line of

The Archæological Survey of Nubia provided a very large series of dislocations and fractured bones showing every possible condition of union, sometimes with evidence of pathological complication.[1]

The mummy of the Pharaoh Rameses V reveals an affection of the skin strongly suggesting small-pox, but the exact diagnosis cannot be established with certainty.   The whole appearance of the remains of this king suggest that he was in a very unhealthy condition at the time of his death, and there is evidence of a marked degree of hydrocele.[2]

In the mummy of a woman of the Byzantine period from Nubia, a case of adhesions of an old appendicitis was found, and in the same necropolis a case of pleural adhesions was also brought to light. The left lung, collapsed and shrunken, was firmly bound to the chest wall by a series of old adhesions.   Cases of intestinal and vaginal prolapsus and a case of vaginal cyst were also found in Nubia.[3]   An instance of uterine disease was recognized in a mummy of the Persian Period by A. B. Granville over a century ago.[4]

Apart from the evidence of disease furnished by the actual human remains that have been found in such enormous numbers in Egypt and Nubia, the

least resistance, that it broke later through the tip of the process, tracked down the neck into the thorax and thus caused death ' (p. 63).

[1] *Report*, pp. 293–342.

[2] G. Elliot Smith, *The Royal Mummies* (Cairo 1912), p. 91 and Pl. 56.

[3] *Report*, pp. 267–268.

[4] *Philosophical Transactions*, 1825 ; cf. W. R. Dawson, *Journal of Egyptian Archæology*, Vol. xi (1925), p. 77.

PLATE IV

(b) STATUE OF KHNUMHOTP

AN ACHONDROPLASTIC DWARF WHO LIVED IN THE
VIth DYNASTY (Cairo Museum)

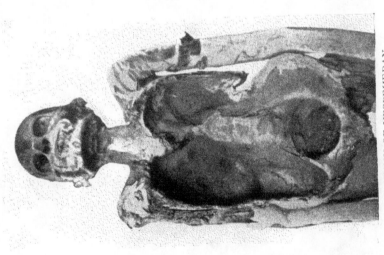

(a) MUMMY OF NESPEHERAN

A PRIEST OF THE XXIst DYNASTY, WITH THE SPINAL
CONDITION KNOWN AS POTT'S DISEASE

pictures, bas-reliefs and statues of Egypt have preserved records of several cases of medical interest.   There is, for instance, a stela of the Nineteenth or Twentieth Dynasty (*circa* 1350–1200 B.C.), now in the Glyptothek ny Carlsberg, Copenhagen, that shows the deformity of the leg of an adult man resulting from infantile paralysis. This stela, although of Egyptian workmanship, commemorates a Semitic settler in Egypt, and the deity invoked in the inscription is the Syrian goddess Astarte.

I recently collected and published a large number of instances of dwarfs and other deformed persons from the Egyptian monuments.   Amongst the cases, they were many of achondroplasia, and a certain number of double talipes varus, talipes equinus, and talipes equinovarus.   There are also cases of Pott's disease, steatopygia, lordosis, and a condition that seems to be adiposis dolorosa, or Dercum's disease.[1]

One of the most interesting pathological cases from ancient Egypt is a condition of affairs revealed by the bones of the heretic king Akhenaten (Amenophis IV) of the Eighteenth Dynasty.   His portraits display consistently a strange bodily contour.   He had large feminine hips, a protruding belly, an elongated skull and jaw.   This peculiar physiognomy is indicated in his skeleton.   When Prof. Elliot Smith examined the skeleton in 1907, the anatomical evidence seemed to point to an age of about 23 years, or at the most 30, if the process of development had been exceptionally delayed, whereas the historical evidence demands an

[1] W. R. Dawson, 'Pygmies, Dwarfs and Hunchbacks in Ancient Egypt', *Annals of Medical History*, Vol. ix (New York 1927), pp. 315–326 and figs. 1–53.

age of at least 30, and in all probability 36 years. Prof. Elliot Smith says:

' In considering this difficult problem I naturally turned to consider those pathological conditions which might cause delay in the union of the epiphyses. Of these the most likely seemed to be the syndrome described by Froelich in 1900, now known as dystrophia adiposo-genitalis. In cases presenting this condition, cases have been recorded in which the bones at 36 years of age reveal the condition which in the normal individual they show at 22 or 23, so that this suggested one possibility of bringing the anatomical evidence into harmony with the historical data. In support of this solution there are the very peculiar anatomical features of Akhnaton [Akhenaten] when alive, which have been made familiar to us by a large series of contemporary portraits. Forty years ago archæologists were puzzled by the pictures of this Pharaoh, and it was suggested that he was a woman masquerading as a man. In the light of our present knowledge, however, they seem to be quite distinctive of Froelich's syndrome and afford valuable support to the suggestion that this was the real cause for the delay in the fusion of the epiphyses. In addition to this, the skull—both the brain-case and the face—reveals certain important peculiarities. There is a slight degree of hydrocephalus, such as is often associated with Froelich's syndrome, and also an overgrowth of the mandible, such as may result from interference with the pituitary. The full solution of this problem cannot be made until the bones are submitted to a much fuller investigation than I was permitted to make in 1907.' [1]

---

[1] G. Elliot Smith, *Cambridge University Medical Society Magazine*, Vol. iv, No. 1 (1926), pp. 37-38.

CHAPTER VII

DRUGS AND DOSES

THE Egyptians employed great numbers of different drugs in their prescriptions, but the same difficulty arises when dealing with these as has already been mentioned in connection with the maladies, namely, our inability to identify many of them. Some hundreds of ingredients are mentioned in the prescriptions, and they are derived from the animal, vegetable and mineral kingdoms. Most of the animals it is possible to identify : usually their fat, flesh or blood is employed, but, if small enough, the whole animal is used. Amongst the mammals put to therapeutic uses are the ox, ass, goat, gazelle, deer, oryx, pig, hippopotamus, lion, mouse, bat [1] and hedgehog ; amongst the birds are ducks and geese of various kinds, the swallow,[2] the vulture, the bee-eater, hoopoe and several other species of uncertain identity. Frogs, lizards, snakes, tortoises [3] and several different kinds of fishes, together with a number of invertebrate animals, also appear

[1] I have traced the history of various animal drugs in a series of articles published in the *American Druggist* in 1926 : the Mouse in the issue of February, and the Bat in that of July.

[2] *American Druggist*, April 1926.   [3] *Ibid.*, August 1926.

in the prescriptions. In the case of vegetable drugs, the number is very large, but it is not possible at present to identify with certainty more than a relatively small proportion of the very large number whose names appear in the prescriptions. Therapeutic use was made of the whole plant, or its leaves, pods, fruit, seeds, juice, rind, roots or resin. The same difficulties of identification arise in the case of the mineral drugs.

The vehicles for liquid doses are usually water, milk, honey, wine or beer. For emollients and ointments, honey, gums, resins and fats of various kinds are used, goose-grease being especially frequent. Dry medicines are pounded, ground or dissolved, and some of the remedies are boiled, warmed or cooled as the case may be. Medicaments for external use are usually applied to the affected part by rubbing, bandaging or as poultices. Pills, pastilles and suppositories were also in use. Directions are often given in the prescriptions as to the manner of administering the medicine, that is to say whether to be taken night and morning, before or after food, etc. The quantities of each drug are meticulously specified in the prescriptions, minute fractional notation being employed, and from this it may be inferred that considerable care was used in dispensing (see below, p. 129).

In considering the uses to which the various drugs were put, it is impossible, owing to their immense number, to do more than select a few as specimens. Amongst the animals used in medicine mention has already been made of the deer. Now the horns, hoofs and bones of various animals, sometimes ground and sometimes calcined, are not infrequently mentioned in the prescriptions. Amongst these occur the horns or antlers of the stag, and a number of prescriptions exists in which the substance obtained by pounding or burning these antlers is therapeutically applied : such is the earliest use of hartshorn, a drug with a long history.[1] In the Ebers Papyrus is a prescription ' to cool a head that suffers pain ', and in it hartshorn is one of ten drugs to be brayed, mixed with water and applied to the head.[2] In another papyrus, hartshorn is used in preparations to drive out the demon that causes disease. In one of these it is used with the legs of a bird, the hair of an ass and the dung of swallows and geese, with the direction ' fumigate the person with it '[3] ; and in another, hartshorn is mixed with the dung of the cat, crocodile and swallow for a similar fumigation.[4] In a prescription ' to drive out painful swellings that afflict a man in winter and in summer ', hartshorn is employed as an ointment, to be applied to the two sides of the patient, the horn being brayed with flour and incense mixed with sweet ale.[5] In another prescription ground hartshorn is used, apparently as a fumigation, for an affection of the ears.[6] In later times, hartshorn still appears in an Egyptian papyrus of the Christian period.[7]

[1] I have traced the history of this drug from ancient to modern times in the *American Druggist*, March 1926.

[2] *Ebers Papyrus*, 48, 15–17.

[3] *Berlin Medical Papyrus*, 6, 9.

[4] *Ibid.*, 6, 10.   [5] *Ibid.*, 11, 11–12.

[6] *Louvre Ostracon*, 3255, lines 1–2.

[7] E. Chassinat, *Un Papyrus Médical Copte* (Cairo 1921), p. 55.

However fantastic these remedies may appear to-day, hartshorn is a valuable medicine which was used by the Greeks, Syrians and Arabs in ancient times and is frequent in the medical works of Western Europe throughout medieval times to the present day. Although actual horns are no longer used, the name 'hartshorn' has survived in modern pharmacy. 'Spirits of hartshorn', a term now used to designate an aqueous solution of ammonia, was originally applied to the ammoniacal liquor obtained by distillation of horn shavings, and in modern preparations, calcium phosphate is added to represent that formed originally from calcined horns.

Mention may now be made of a few of the vegetable drugs. Pomegranates, for instance, were cultivated in Egypt in very early times, and the tree is frequently mentioned in the inscriptions, and actual fruits have been found in the tombs.[1] In the Ebers Papyrus we find the rind of the pomegranate beaten up and taken in water as a vermifuge,[2] a use to which it was put for many centuries in many different countries. It was put to other uses that are closely paralleled in the Assyrian, Greek and Arabic medical texts.[3] Dill, coriander, cumin,[4] caraway, fenugreek [5]

[1] I have traced the history of the pomegranate in medicine in the *American Druggist*, December 1925.

[2] *Ebers Papyrus*, 16, 15–18 ; 19, 19–21.

[3] References are given in my paper, *American Druggist*, December 1925.

[4] For the history of Dill and Cumin in medicine, see my papers in the *American Druggist*, June and September 1926.

[5] Identified by W. R. Dawson, *Journal of Egyptian Archæology*, Vol. xii (1926), pp. 240–241. The Egyptian name of the plant is 'Hairs of the Earth'.

and other herbs familiar in later times for their medicinal properties, are amongst the many drugs employed by the Egyptians in therapeutics. Onions and figs also play an obtrusive part in the medical and magical texts.[1]

It has frequently been stated that the mandrake was used by the Egyptians in medicine. There is no evidence, however, in support of this assertion. The word *didi*, thought to mean 'mandrake', was identified with the Hebrew *dudaim*, the 'love-apples' of the Old Testament : actually, however, *didi* is the name of a mineral (hæmatite), and not of a plant.

Some fruits of the mandrake were discovered amongst the floral remains in the tomb of Tutankhamen, but their use here was decorative, not medicinal. Until these fruits were found, there was no evidence whatever that the plant was even known to the Egyptians. Tutankhamen's mandrakes were evidently imported from Western Asia, where the plant is not uncommon and was used by the Assyrians as a drug : it is not, and never has been, a native of the Nile Valley.[2]

Another familiar drug of vegetable origin, used by the Egyptians, is castor-oil. Herodotus, Diodorus Siculus, Strabo, Pliny and others relate that the Egyptians cultivated the castor-oil plant and obtained from its seeds an oil that they used in their lamps as an illuminant. These writers, and others such as

[1] For the history of the Onion and the Fig, see *American Druggist*, January and October 1926.

[2] I have discussed the mandrake problem fully in a paper : ' The Substance called *Didi* by the Egyptians', *Journal of the Royal Asiatic Society*, July 1927, pp. 497–503.

Dioscorides, Oribasius and many more, state that the Egyptian name of the plant is *kiki*. There is indeed an Egyptian herb of similar sound, ⊔ 𓅐 ⊔ 𓅐 𓆱 *k'ak'a*, but this is certainly not the same as the plant called κίκι by the Greeks. The Egyptian word for castor-oil is *degam*.[1] This *degam* was used as an illuminant, and an inscription of the Twenty-sixth Dynasty in the Louvre states: ' I have given oil of *degam* for the lighting of the temples '. The plant was used in medicine, and in the following quotations, to avoid the repeated use of the cumbrous tripartite ' castor-oil plant', I will use its botanical name, *Ricinus*. The prescriptions in which *Ricinus* occurs are as follows :—

    a. ' Another for purging the belly and for expelling the fæces from the belly of a person. *Ricinus* seeds : chew, swallow with beer, until all that is in the belly comes away.' [2]

    b. ' Another for driving away pain. Ointment made from the seeds of *Ricinus*. Anoint therewith the person who is afflicted with sores that emit a foul discharge. . . . [3] The sores will disappear by anointing thus for 10 days, anointing very early in the morning

[1] The words *kiki*, *degam*, and the Coptic, Arabic and other synonyms and derivatives will form the subject of a detailed memoir shortly to be published. The problem is very complicated and its elucidation involves an amount of technical detail which would be out of place here.

[2] *Ebers Papyrus*, 8, 12–16.

[3] The text is very corrupt and the translation only conjectural for the most part. The words omitted are unintelligible. The sense, however, is quite clear.

in order to expel them. A true remedy;
[proved] millions of times.' [1]

c. 'Beginning of the prescriptions for driving away
khensyt [2] from the head. *Ricinus* seeds, 1
[part]; fat, 1; olive oil, 1. Make into one
mass, anoint therewith every day.' [3]

d. 'Another for driving away suffering from any
member of a person. *Ricinus* seeds: Crush,
mix with honey, bandage therewith.' [4]

e. In a prescription 'to drive away the influence
of a god or a goddess, a male poison or a
female poison, a dead man or a dead woman',
etc., *Ricinus* seeds, mixed with beans and
other seeds, are used in a fumigation. [5]

f. At the end of a long incantation for burns, the
manual rite is, 'bandage it [the burned limb]
with a leaf of *Ricinus*'. [6]

g. A prescription for treatment of *temyt* [an
unidentified disease] begins with 'fruit of
Ricinus': most of the other drugs are
unidentified, but the mixture contains dates
and honey, and is for external application. [7]

In addition to these actual prescriptions, the Ebers
Papyrus contains a very interesting passage relating

---

[1] *Ebers*, 27, 11–14.
[2] An unidentified disease: an affection of the scalp, possibly alopecia.
[3] *Ebers*, 64, 14–15=*Hearst Medical Papyrus*, 2, 8–9.
[4] *Ebers*, 76, 16–18.
[5] *Berlin Medical Papyrus*, 5, 9–11. The text is too badly mutilated to allow of a continuous translation.
[6] *London Medical Papyrus*, 14, 13–14.
[7] *Hearst Medical Papyrus*, 11, 11–12.

to *Ricinus*.   It deals with the medical properties of
the plant (some of them already mentioned in the
above-quoted prescriptions) and is the earliest known
fragment of a Herbal.   This passage is unique and
differs in character from all the other contents of
the manuscript.   The remainder of the papyrus consists for the most part of ailments and diseases, that
is to say the classification is pathological, whereas
this fragment is taken from a collection in which the
classification is pharmaceutical, i.e. the drugs are
enumerated and for each its appropriate therapeutic
uses given.   Unhappily the fragment is very corrupt,
and although it would be hard to justify grammati-
cally the whole of the rendering given below, fortunately its sense is perfectly clear.

' List of the virtues of *Ricinus* : it was found in an ancient
book concerning the things beneficial to mankind.

If its rind be brayed in water and applied to a head that
suffers, it will be cured immediately as if it had never been
affected.

If a few of its seeds be chewed with beer by a person who
is constipated, it will expel the fæces from the body of that
person.

The hair of woman will be made to grow by means of its
seeds.   Bray, mix, and apply with grease.   Let the woman
anoint her head with it.

Its oil is made from its seeds.   For anointing sores that
emit a foul discharge. . . .[1]   Anoint very early in the morning
in order to drive them [the sores] away.   A true remedy.
[Proved] millions of times.' [2]

---

[1] The omitted words are the same as those in prescription
b, above.

[2] *Ebers Papyrus*, 47, 15–48, 3.   I have discussed this passage fully in a forthcoming memoir on the origin of the Herbal.

Amongst the mineral drugs are found minium, alum, salt, hæmatite, carbonate of soda, natron and other substances, but many of these have not yet been identified.

It will be convenient now to give some specimens of Egyptian prescriptions from the medical papyri.

' Another for expelling excrement and sickness from the abdomen of a person.

White gum, 1 ; red *tyt,* 1 ; human milk. Mix into one. To be swallowed by the man.' [1]

This is evidently a medicine for constipation. The following is perhaps for gripes :

' Another for expelling illness from the side of the abdomen. *Efai*-plant, 1 ; dates, 1 ; cook in fat. Bandage therewith.' [2]

There are many prescriptions for ' killing worms '; here are two specimens :

' Another. Seeds of *nozem*-tree, 1 ; milk, 1 ; honey, 1 ; fenugreek seeds, 1 ; wine, 1. Warm, beat up, eat for 4 days. It purges the body.' [3]

' Another. Fenugreek seeds, 1 ; heart of the *mesha'*-bird, 1 ; honey, 1 ; wine, 1 ; *innk*-plant, 1 ; sweet ale, 1. Make into a cake. Eat for one day.' [4]

Amongst the diseases of the eye, there are many complaints that involve swelling of the eyelids, and this often has the effect of forcing the lashes inwards, thereby causing irritation to the pupil. In such cases the lashes were pulled out, and there are many prescriptions to prevent them from growing again. For this purpose blood was believed to be efficacious.

[1] *Ebers,* 10, 9–14.   [2] *Ebers,* 13, 12–15.
[3] *Ebers,* 22, 13–14.   [4] *Ebers,* 22, 14–15.

'Another for preventing the hair [i.e. lashes] from pricking the eye. Frankincense, 1 ; lizard's blood, 1 ; bat's blood, 1. Clip the hair. Apply until [the eye] is well.' [1]

'Another for preventing the lashes growing on the eyelids after they have been pulled out. Blood of an ox, 1 ; blood of an ass, 1 ; blood of a pig, 1 ; blood of a dog, 1 ; blood of an oryx, 1 ; *mesdem*-salve, 1 ; green ointment, 1. Pound into one with the blood. Apply it to the place of the hair after it has been pulled out. It will not grow again.' [2]

'Another. Bat's blood, 1 ; sherd [lit. " lips "] of a new pot, 1 ; honey, 1. Pound-up, apply it to the place of the hair after it has been pulled out.' [3]

A short passage embodying symptoms and diagnosis may now be quoted, evidently a case of boils :

'If you see a man with a swelling on his neck, who suffers pain on both sides of his neck, and who suffers pain in his head ; the vertebræ of his neck are rigid, so that it is impossible for him [lit. " it does not happen to him "] to look down at his belly, for it hurts him, then you say " He has a swelling on his neck ". You order that he must anoint it with stibium until he is comfortable, immediately.' [4]

For stiffness of the joints, pains in the muscles and for rheumatoid complaints, most of the remedies are compounded on a basis of fat and generally consist of ointments.

'Another for easing [lit. " oiling "] stiffness in any member of a man. Natron, 1 ; grease, the second day, 1 ; hippopotamus fat, 1 ; crocodile fat, 1 ; fat of *adu*-fish, 1 ; fat of silurus fish, 1 ; incense, 1 ; sweet frankincense, 1 ; honey, 1. Warm ; bandage therewith.' [5]

---

[1] *Ebers*, 63, 12–13.   [2] *Ebers*, 63, 14–18.
[3] *Ebers*, 63, 18–19.   [4] *Ebers*, 51, 19–52, 1.
[5] *Ebers*, 82, 7–10.

Mouth-washes were used for ailments of the tongue. There are seven prescriptions for this purpose, from which the following are selected :

'Beginning of the prescriptions for driving out illness from the tongue. Milk: rinse with it, spit it out ' [lit. ' put it on the ground '].[1]

'Another for treating the tongue. Incense, 1 ; cumin, 1 ; *khenty*, 1 ; goose-fat, 1 ; honey, 1 ; water, 1 ; rinse.' [2]

The following prescriptions relate to children :

'To be done for a child who suffers from diarrhœa. Burnt ochre made into a pill. If the child is old [enough], let him eat it in his food. If he is in swaddling-clothes [i.e. very young], let it be rubbed into his nurse's milk [lit. " the milk that his nurse emits "] for 4 days.' [3]

'To know the destiny of a child on the day of its birth. If it says *ny*, it will live ; if it says *mbi*, it will die.' [4]

There is a prescription in which, as written in the manuscript, the strange ingredient ' human gall ' occurs. I have elsewhere given reasons on palæographical grounds, for emending this to ' pig's gall '. The hieratic groups for *rmt*, ' man ', and *rer*, ' pig ', might easily be miscopied in a badly-written manuscript.[5] The prescription is as follows :

'Another prescription for the eye when illness befalls it. Pig's gall, divided into two parts. Put one half with honey, anoint the eye therewith at night ; dry the other half, grind it up, and anoint the eye with it in the morning.' [6]

---

[1] *Ebers*, 85, 16–17.   [2] *Ebers*, 85, 19–20.

[3] *Ebers*, 49, 21–50, 2.

[4] *Ebers*, 97, 13–14. The words *ny* and *mbi* mean ' yes ' and ' no ' respectively.

[5] *Zeitschrift für ägyptische Sprache*, Bd. 60 (1926), pp. 21, 22.

[6] *Ebers*, 61, 12–14.

The emendation proposed is further supported by
the fact that the ancients attached great importance
to the gall of animals as being efficacious for various
affections of the eyes, and Dioscorides mentions the
pig amongst the animals whose gall is especially good
for treating the eyes.[1]

As the medical papyri of Pharaonic times contain
in the aggregate over two thousand prescriptions, it is
difficult to select out of this number a small series
that will convey an adequate impression of their
nature and scope. A great many of the drugs employed are appropriate and rational, but many more
appear to-day as fantastic or repulsive. Many of
them, as already stated, are clearly magical and not
therapeutic in their action: in the gynæcological
cases this is especially noticeable, as the following
examples show :

‘ Directions for a woman who suffers in her eyes so that
she cannot see, and has pains in her neck. You say: “ It
is vaginal discharge affecting her eyes ”. You do thus for
it : fumigate her with incense and fresh fat in her vulva,
fumigate her eyes with the legs of the bee-eater (*Merops
apiaster*), then make her eat the liver of an ass, raw.’ [2]

Some of the recipes embody the principle of sympathetic magic, thus :

‘ Directions for a woman who suffers pain in her vulva when
walking. You say: “ What is the smell that she emits ? ”
If she says to you : “ I emit the smell of burnt meat ”, you

---

[1] Dioscorides, *De Materia Medica*, ii, 96 ; nevertheless
Pliny (*Nat. Hist.*, xxviii, 2) says ‘ oculorum suffusiones felle
hominis sanari ’, a statement attributed by him to Miletus,
but probably ultimately derived from a corrupt Egyptian
manuscript.

[2] *Kahun Medical Papyrus*, lines 1–5 (Case No. 1).

say: "It is *nemsu* (? pustule, cyst) of the vagina". You do thus for it: fumigate her with burnt meat the smell of which she emits.' [1]

' To bring milk to a woman who is nursing a child. Backbone of a silurus fish cooked in fat: rub her backbone with it.' [2]

Some of the medical prescriptions consist of one ingredient only, but most of them have three or four, and in some cases the number of drugs is considerable.[3] Reference has already been made to a preference for rare and bizarre elements: simple and easily obtained drugs are seldom used alone, they are nearly always combined with rarer substances.

By way of comparison with the more ancient prescriptions quoted above, a few taken from the Greek medical papyri found in Egypt and from the demotic and Coptic texts of later times may be added. The following remedies for the ears are extracted from a medical papyrus written in Greek, of the second or third century A.D. :

' Stoppings for the ear against earache. Pound some Egyptian alum and insert into the ear an amount equal to the size of a pea.'

' Another. Anoint a persea leaf and insert.'

' Another. Thoroughly moisten a flock of wool with the gall of an ox, roll up and insert.'

' Another. Pound myrrh and alum in equal quantities and insert.'

---

[1] *Kahun Medical Papyrus*, 5–8 (No. 2).

[2] *Ebers Papyrus*, 97, 10–11.

[3] *Ebers*, 82, 22–83, 8, a prescription for easing the muscles, has 37 ingredients: it ends with the usual rubric, ' mix into one: bandage therewith '.

'Clysters for the ear against earache. Dilute frankincense with very sweet wine and syringe the ear: or use for this purpose the injections described above.'

'Another. Rinse with warm onion juice.'

'Another. Syringe with the gall of a bull, or goat, or sheep, or other similar kind of gall, warmed.'

'Another. The sap of a pine-tree, warmed, to be used in the same way.' [1]

While on the subject of ears, the following, from the London-Leiden Magical Papyrus (third century A.D.) is of particular interest :

'Medicament for an ear that is watery. Salt, heat with good wine; you apply it after cleansing it first. You scrape salt, heat with wine, and apply it for four days.' [2]

This is rational enough, and not so very far removed from the ear-drops composed of boracic powder and spirits of wine prescribed to-day by doctors for aural discharge. The following remedy is magical character :

'Gout. You make the man sit down; you place clay under the feet of the man; you put . . . to it, his feet resting on it; you ask the man, saying, " Has it harkened ? " for three days. Thereafter you take an ant (?), you cook it in oil of henna; you anoint his feet with it. When you have finished, you take Alexandrian figs and dried grapes and potentilla; you pound them with wine; you anoint him besides (?) these; and you blow on him with your mouth.' [3]

---

[1] B. P. Grenfell and A. Hunt, *The Oxyrhynchus Papyri*, Part ii (London 1899), No. 234, pp. 134–136.

[2] *London-Leiden Papyrus*, Verso, 4, 1–5 ; Griffith and Thompson, *The Demotic Magical Papyrus*, Vol. i (London 1904), p. 175.

[3] *Ibid.*, Verso, 8, 1–8 ; Griffith and Thompson, *op. cit.*, p. 181.

The following prescriptions are selected from a miscellaneous collection of remedies in an Egyptian papyrus written in Greek of the early part of the first century A.D. :

'The Yellow Salve for discharges, wounds, bruises and weals: calamine, 4 dr.; white lead, 8 dr.; fine meal, 4 dr.; purified schist, 1 dr.; saffron, 1 dr.; opium, 3 ob.; gum, 4 dr.; water.'

'Styptic: use pounded rock alum, and it will stop [the blood] at once.'

'To stop nose-bleeding: mix frankincense with onion juice and apply the juice inside.'

'For sores in the nose: rub yellow orpiment smooth, then lay the man on his back and treat him, or use black hellebore in the same way.'

'Draught for liver-patients: sweet flag, 1 dr.; opoponax, 1 ob.; spikenard, 1 ob.; parsnip, 2 dr.; to be drunk slowly with raisin wine or honey.'

'Soporific: henbane . . . anise, 1 dr.; opium, 4 ob.; mix and administer.' [1]

Finally, from the great Coptic medical papyrus of Meshaîkh (ninth or tenth century A.D.) the following examples may be selected from the 237 prescriptions it contains :

'A good powder for the eyes. Armenian borax, 10 obols; white lead, 2 ob.; pepper, 1 ob.; ginger, 1 ob.; verdigris, ⅔ ob.; starch, 2 ob.; sal-ammoniac, 1 ob. Pound them well, strain through a fine sieve: apply to the eyes that are dim and they will become quite clear.' [2]

---

[1] A. S. Hunt, *The Oxyrhynchus Papyri*, Part viii (London 1911), No. 1088, pp. 110–115.

[2] Coptic papyrus published by E. Chassinat, *Un Papyrus Médical Copte* (Cairo 1921), lines 24–26 (No. 11).

'Ear that suffers acutely. Opium; calf's fat; milk. Melt them down together, warm them, and apply to the ear. The pain will stop immediately. But do not administer this remedy to a man until you have received your fee.'[1]

This infallible cure evidently worked so quickly that the physician is advised to collect his fee in advance!

'A tooth to be extracted with instruments [lit. "iron"]. Hellebore of good quality and gall; apply to the region of the cheek where the molar is that you wish to extract, and you will be astonished!'[2]

'Anyone who has worms in him. Camomile; mastic; rue; wine; pound them, mix with the wine, and let him drink it.'[3]

'Powder that cauterizes quickly: iris, 4 dr.; vetch, 4 dr.; flakes of copper, 2 dr.; aristolochia, 4 dr.; roasted resin, 16 dr.; incense, 2 dr.; white vitriol, 20 dr. Pound them well; make into a powder; apply.'[4]

'Head affected with itch. Cress seed; mustard; pound with vinegar; apply.'[5]

'Head of a small child affected with itch. Sycomore latex and Ethiopian salve: apply, and the mischief will cease.'[6]

Sycomore latex, or as it is written 'milk of Sycomore', is often employed in the ancient papyri.[7]

'Purulent itch (or scab). Roast some fennel, grind it well with sour vinegar until it has suitable consistence:

---

[1] Coptic papyrus published by E. Chassinat, *Un Papyrus Médical Copte* (Cairo 1921), lines 242–3; No. 114.

[2] *Ibid.*, ll. 305-6; No. 151.

[3] *Ibid.*, l. 324; No. 166.   [4] *Ibid.*, ll. 283–4; No. 139.

[5] *Ibid.*, l. 121; No. 60.   [6] *Ibid.*, l. 72; No. 38.

[7] E.g. *Ebers Papyrus*, 69, 8; 69, 13; *Hearst Papyrus*, 3, 8; 10, 17; *Berlin Medical Papyrus*, 8, 1; *London Medical Papyrus*, 15, 12; etc.

anoint the patient with it. Leave it to dry, then wash off with warm water : the affection will cease. If you also apply this remedy to a creeping ulcer, it will dry it up.' [1]

' White plaster for treating persistent wounds, and bites of dogs or men : it is very good. Burnt lead, 8 oz. ; wax, 2 lb. ; oil, 1 lb. ; pine resin, 2 lb. ; sweet wine, 10 measures. Melt them over the fire ; apply.' [2]

Human bites were thought by the ancients to be very dangerous, and the Ebers and Hearst Papyri devote several prescriptions to their treatment. The classical writers frequently allude to human bites ; Oribasius,[3] for instance, has a special chapter on the subject, and it is often referred to by Avicenna, by Pliny and by medieval writers.

The specimens of medical prescriptions quoted in this chapter range over a period of thirty centuries. In the last chapter some instances will be given of the survival of ancient remedies, but in the meantime a brief survey may be made of Assyrian medicine, the records of which are second only to those of Egypt in antiquity.

[1] *Coptic Papyrus*, lines 265–6 ; No. 127.
[2] *Ibid.*, ll. 349–351 ; No. 187.
[3] *Euporista*, iii, 71, πρὸς ἀνθρωποδήκτους.

CHAPTER VIII

ASSYRIAN MEDICINE

ACCORDING to Herodotus the Babylonians had no physicians, and they brought their sick into the market-places in order that passers-by might confer with them upon their symptoms, in the hope that the patient might elicit from someone who had been similarly afflicted, advice as to how to proceed to effect a cure.[1] Whether this be true or not, their neighbours the Assyrians possessed considerable medical knowledge of which a mass of documentary evidence has come down to us.

Until lately, but few Assyrian medical texts had been published. From their nature, being, as they are, inscribed in cuneiform characters on brittle and often fragmentary clay tablets, these texts are often damaged and extremely difficult to read. In the ruins of the royal library to King Ashurbanipal (668–626 B.C.) at Nineveh (Kouyunjik) thousands of clay tablets have been found. In the reign of this monarch, Assyrian literature may be said to have reached its high-water mark, both as regards quantity and merit. From this famous site vast quantities of historical, literary, religious, magical, astronomical

[1] *Herodotus*, i, 197.

and medical texts have been recovered.[1] It is to Dr. R. Campbell Thompson of Oxford that we are indebted for most of our knowledge of Assyrian medicine and magic.[2] In 1906 he commenced a systematic study of the Assyrian medical texts, and soon came to the conclusion that the material must be worked over as a whole, and that to continue to publish isolated fragments would lead to no solid result. Accordingly he set to work to collect, transcribe and study this great mass of tablets, a task that occupied many years, and that was interrupted by the war. Some 660 tablets in the British Museum, nearly all of them previously unpublished, were examined and collated, and the cuneiform texts issued in a series of 107 plates by Dr. Campbell Thompson in 1923.[3] Having published the texts, the next step was to translate them; but before doing so, another and very important matter had first to be settled, and this is best described in the author's own words:

'The work of editing so many texts is a long business; and it became obvious, when I set about them again after my return from the War, that the old method of leaving the vegetable drugs unidentified, or translated haphazard, would lead us nowhere. No satisfactory translation of these texts was possible until the plants had been in some measure worked out; and to this end I spent a large part of two years at work on the 250 vegetable drugs known to the Assyrian botanists.'[4]

---

[1] See G. Maspero, *The Passing of the Empires* (London, 1900), pp. 462 ff.

[2] In addition to his medical works mentioned below, see *Semitic Magic* (London 1908). (Vol. iii of Luzac's Oriental Religions Series.)

[3] *Assyrian Medical Texts from the Originals in the British Museum* (Oxford 1923).   [4] *Ibid.*, Preface, p. iv.

The results of these labours are contained in a thick volume that Dr. Campbell Thompson published in 1924.[1] In this work many wrong identifications were corrected, and a large series of plants identified for the first time. A year later, a second volume appeared dealing with the mineral drugs and with the extensive chemical knowledge of the Assyrians.[2] At the same time the translations of the texts were begun, and this work is still in progress.[3]

Thanks to these painstaking labours, the student of ancient Assyrian medicine is in a far better position to investigate his subject than the student of Egyptian medicine, for in the latter case, a great part of this preliminary work still remains to be done.

From the material now at our disposal, we can at once perceive that there is a great similarity between the Assyrian and the Egyptian medical texts : both are strange mixtures of rational therapeutics with magical spells and incantations. It seems evident that the conceptions of the two peoples concerning the nature of disease were essentially similar. There is some difference, however, in the method of setting out the prescriptions. In the Egyptian papyri, as we have seen, the name of the ailment is usually stated in the title : thus ' prescription for driving away swellings ', ' prescription for a pain in the head ', ' prescription for an ear that discharges ', and so on.

---

[1] *The Assyrian Herbal* (London 1924).

[2] *On the Chemistry of the Ancient Assyrians* (London 1925).

[3] Up to the present two parts have appeared in the *Proceedings of the Royal Society of Medicine*, Vol. xvii (1924), pp. 1-34 ; Vol. xix (1926), pp. 29-78 [Section of the History of Medicine].

A few of the Egyptian remedies begin with the words : 'if you see', or 'if you examine' a man in such and such condition, and this conditional opening with the word 'if' is the usual method of presenting the remedies in the Assyrian texts. Instead of giving the disease a name, the texts usually describe its symptoms, thus : 'If a man's head has a scab', you shall do so and so ; or 'If a man's teeth hurt, you shall take' such and such drugs and apply them ; similarly, 'If the accident of a blow has fallen upon him', etc. Another point of difference lies in the fact that in the majority of Egyptian prescriptions, the quantities of each drug used are stated : [1] this detail is lacking in the Assyrian texts.

Interspersed amongst the Assyrian prescriptions (as also among the Egyptian) there are incantations, and often also the 'Ritual' to be performed when the spell is recited. These, of course, are exact parallels of the *oral rites* and *manual rites* to which reference was made when discussing Egyptian magic in Chapter IV. The following is a specimen of an incantation for the eyes.

'Incantation for a sick eye.
'Ritual for this : this is for red wool, a thread thou shalt spin, tie seven knots, as thou tiest them recite the charm, bind on his sick eye.
'Charm. O failing eyes, O painful eyes, O eyes sundered

---

[1] In the specimen prescriptions quoted in the last chapter, I avoided those that involve fractional notation, as it is outside our present purpose to enter into the subject of Egyptian weights and measures. Most of the drugs are measured in terms of the *hekat*, and the fractions of it are usually $\frac{1}{2}$, $\frac{1}{4}$, $\frac{1}{8}$, $\frac{1}{32}$, and $\frac{1}{64}$. See T. E. Peet, *The Rhind Mathematical Papyrus* (Liverpool 1923), p. 25.

by a dam of blood! Why do ye fail, why do ye hurt? Why has the dust of the river come nigh you, or the spathe of the date-palm whereof ye have chanced to catch the pollen which the fertilizer hath been shaking? Have I invited you, Come to me? I have not invited you,[1] come not to me, or even the first wind, the second wind, the third wind, the fourth wind cometh to you.'[2]

The use in magic of a thread with seven knots, which is frequent in these texts, is paralleled as we have already seen, in the Egyptian magical texts. The following is a spell for blindness:

'Incantation of a sick eye.

'Ritual for this: as before.

'Charm. In Heaven the wind blew and brought blindness to the eye of the man: from the distant heavens the wind blew and brought blindness to the eye of the man. Unto the sick eye it brought blindness; of this man his eye is troubled, his eye is pained. The man weepeth grievously for himself.

'Of this man, his sickness Ea hath espied and said, "take pounded roses, perform the charm of the Deep, and bind the eye of the man". When Ea toucheth the eye of the man

---

[1] The phrasing of this part of the incantation may be compared with that of an Egyptian spell: 'Dost thou come to kiss this child? I suffer thee not to kiss him. Dost thou come to soothe him? I suffer thee not to soothe him. Dost thou come to harm him? I suffer thee not to harm him. Dost thou come to carry him off? I suffer thee not to carry him off,' etc. *Berlin Papyrus*, 3027, 2, 1–3.

[2] *Proceedings of the Royal Society of Medicine* (hereinafter cited as *Proceedings*), Vol. xvii (1924), p. 31, No. 8. In this and the other quotations from Dr. Campbell Thompson's translations, I have omitted the notes of interrogation and other critical marks, in order to facilitate the reading. References to the source are given in every case.

with his holy hand, let the wind which hath brought woe to the eye of the man go forth ! ' [1]

The treatment of disease by magical means presupposes a belief in a supernatural causative agent. Some illnesses are caused, as has just been seen, by an ' ill-wind ', others are the work of evil spirits or demons. Amongst the incantations, again, there is one called ' Charm against the Hand of a Ghost ',[2] and in another, toothache is attributed to the anger of a dead man whose funerary offerings have been neglected.[3] The efficacy of drugs was attributed to, or at least enhanced by, magical rites. Before passing on to the prescriptions, one further incantation may be quoted, as it embodies the principle that like influences like.

' Charm.   Sound front, sound back, smitten front, smitten back. . . . Flesh multiplieth flesh, blood produceth blood, dung createth dung ! Perform, O Gula, the high Charm of Life ! Let them bring nigh the cataplasms, which thou hast arranged, and grant recovery ! Recite the charm E . NU . ŠUB.' [4]

As has already been mentioned, the Assyrian medical texts are very fragmentary, and although the general sense of most of them is easily understood, comparatively few are sufficiently undamaged to be suitable for quotation. The following selection of

[1] *Proceedings*, Vol. xvii, p. 32, Nos. 10 and 11.
[2] *Semitic Magic*, p. 35.
[3] *Proceedings*, Vol. xix, p. 59, No. 4.
[4] *Proceedings*, Vol. xvii, p. 28, No. 25. With this spell compare the Egyptian spell published by Dr. A. H. Gardiner, *Theban Ostraca* (Toronto and London 1913), pp. 13–15, No. C. 1.

specimens is therefore quite arbitrary, and is made from the prescriptions in the best state of preservation :

' If a man's eyes are sick and full of blood, unguents only irritating the blood, blood and tears coming forth from the eyes, a film closing over the pupils of his eyes, tears turning to film, to look oppressing him : thou shall beat leaves of tamarisk, steep them in strong vinegar, leave them out under the stars ; in the morning (i.e. on the morrow) thou shalt squeeze them in a helmet : white alum, storax, " Akkadian Salt ", fat, cornflour, nigella, " gum of copper ", separately shalt thou bray : thou shalt take equal parts of them, put them together ; pour them into the helmet in which thou hast squeezed the tamarisk ; in curd and *šuniš*-mineral thou shalt knead it, and open his eyelids with a finger and put it in his eyes. While his eyes contain dimness, his eyes thou shalt smear, and for nine days thou shalt do this.' [1]

This prescription is followed by three alternative preparations to be similarly used : here again we have an analogy with Egyptian prescriptions, for in the latter, in nearly every case, a number of alternative remedies is given for each complaint. The text just quoted is almost entirely therapeutic, the only magical element being the direction to leave the medicine under the stars, i.e. to subject it to the magical influence of the stars. Amongst the shorter prescriptions for the eyes, the following may be noted :

' Thou shalt disembowel a yellow frog, mix its gall in curd, apply to his eyes.' [2]

' Blood from a pig's heart thou shalt pour into his eyes.' [3]

' If a man's eyes are full of blood, thou shalt bray yellow sulphide of arsenic in curd, apply . . .' [4]

---

[1] *Proceedings*, Vol. xvii, pp. 28, 29, No. 31.
[2] *Ibid.*, p. 23, No. 13.
[3] *Ibid.*, p. 27, No. 34.   [4] *Ibid.*, p. 26, No. 31.

There are many incantations and prescriptions for toothache. Probably in Assyria, as in Egypt, dental troubles were frequent.[1] The Egyptians believed that the cause, or one of the causes, of toothache, was the gnawing of a worm, and in Assyria the same belief is found: it is very widespread and has persisted until recent times.[2] In this connection the following incantation for toothache is particularly interesting, both from the magical and the mythological points of view:

'Charm. After Anu made the heavens, the heavens made the earth, the earth made the rivers, the rivers made the canals, the canals made the marsh, the marsh made the Worm. The Worm came weeping unto Samas, came unto Ea, her tears flowing: "What wilt thou give me for my food, what wilt thou give me to destroy?" "I will give thee dried figs and apricots." "Forsooth, what are these dried figs to me, or apricots? Set me amid the teeth, and let me dwell in the gums, that I may destroy the blood of the teeth, and of the gums chew their marrow. So shall I hold the latch of the door." "Since thou hast said this, O Worm, may Ea smite thee with his mighty fist!"'[3]

There is a very large collection of remedies for various affections of the mouth and nose. Some of these ailments are evidently ulceration or are connected with catarrh.

'If a man's nose and mouth hold foetor . . . thou shalt roll up a linen pledget, bray Salicornia-alkali (?), powdered alum, . . ., ammi, alum; sprinkle the pledget of linen with

---

[1] See above, p. 105.

[2] Cf. 'What! sigh for the toothache? Where is but a humour or a worm.' *Much Ado About Nothing*, Act iii, Sc. 2.

[3] *Proceedings*, Vol. xix, p. 59.

oil . . . manna green thou shalt bruise [a mutilated passage follows enumerating various drugs, which] thou shalt reduce, bray, mix in oil, let him drink and he shall recover.' [1]

' Thou shalt bray powdered alum and apply it to his tooth ; let him lick the upper stone of a *Lolium* mill, and he shall recover.' [2]

' Thou shalt slit a leek, rub on the root of his tooth, and he shall recover.' [3]

' When a man's mouth and nostrils hold foetor, thou shalt bray alum, roll up a pledget of linen, sprinkle it with oil, gather up the alum on it, put it in his nostrils ; with pounded powdered alum . . . thou shalt rub his nostrils until blood appears. Thou shalt do this for three days, on the fourth manna green thou shalt press and take its juice, two sheckels of oil add, apply and he shall recover.' [4]

The Assyrians were skilled in the preparation of medicines : the extent of their knowledge may be gauged from the long lists of vegetable and mineral drugs and their uses that Dr. Campbell Thompson has drawn up. Whilst, as already indicated, magic played a conspicuous part in the treatment of disease, there is no doubt that the Assyrians had an extensive knowledge of the true values of many drugs, and the greater number of them employed in the prescriptions is, to some extent at least, wholesome and rational.

In concluding this short chapter, it may be mentioned that the tablets from Kouyunjik, which form the basis of this brief summary, all date from the seventh century B.C., but there is evidence that they are derived from much older originals, from their similarity to the medical texts from Ashur, which are some centuries older.

[1] *Proceedings*, Vol. xix, p. 64, No. 11.
[2] *Ibid.*, p. 65, No. 32.
[3] *Ibid.*, p. 65, No. 34.   [4] *Ibid.*, p. 66, No. 18.

CHAPTER IX

THE SURVIVAL OF ANCIENT MEDICINE
Conclusion

WHEN Hippocrates and the great physicians of Greece arose, whose work infused new life into the science of medicine, they did not extinguish the ancient medical lore that had held sway before their time. Much of it survived and spread far and wide, and the Greeks themselves borrowed not a little from the medicine of Egypt and Assyria.

In classical times, the Egyptians had a great reputation for their medical knowledge. Herodotus relates that in Egypt all places abounded with medical practitioners each of whom was a specialist, applying himself to the study of one section of medicine. ' Some physicians are for the eyes, others for the head, others for the teeth, others for the parts about the belly, and others for internal disorders.' [1] The same writer tells us that Cyrus sent to Egypt for an oculist,[2] and that Darius believed that the Egyptians had the highest reputation for their skill in the art of healing.[3] Homer refers to the current opinion that the Egyptians had more skill in medicine than any other race,[4]

[1] *Herodotus,* ii, 84. [2] *Ibid.,* iii, 1.
[3] *Ibid.,* iii, 129. [4] *Odyssey,* iv, 227.

135

and other classical writers have spoken of them in similar terms.

Medicine, as indicated in the foregoing chapters, was in Egypt closely connected with magic and religion,[1] but the Egyptians had no special deity of medicine until late times, when a famous physician and sage who had lived in the time of the Third Dynasty (about 2980 B.C.) was posthumously raised to semi-divine status, and ultimately, in the time of the Ptolemies, became the god of medicine. This was Imhotep, who was called by the Greeks Imouthes, and identified by them with Asklepios, or Æsculapius, their own god of healing.[2] Similar honours were paid posthumously to another famous sage who had been a minister under the Pharaoh Amenophis III, of the Eighteenth Dynasty. This sage, Amenophis, the son of Hapu,[3] was not in his lifetime particularly associated with medicine, but in Ptolemaic times he appears side by side with Imhotep in the bas-reliefs that cover the walls of several of the temples built by the Ptolemies. In the last centuries of the pre-Christian era, these temples were resorted to by the sick who implored the boon of restoration to health from these two deified men who were then accounted as gods with special powers of healing. At an earlier period

[1] This association is common amongst primitive peoples. See W. H. R. Rivers, *Medicine, Magic and Religion* (London 1924).

[2] This famous personage has lately been made the subject of an admirable monograph in which is collected all the information available concerning him. *Imhotep*, by Dr. J. B. Hurry, 2nd ed. (Oxford 1928).

[3] W. R. Dawson, ' Amenophis the Son of Hapu ', *Ægyptus*, Vol. vii (Milan 1926), pp. 113–138.

the god Amun, and several of the minor gods of Thebes, wrought miraculous cures, and many votive tablets, offered by grateful patients, have been found.

If in earlier times the Egyptians had a god of medicine, that god was Thoth, to whom was attributed the invention of writing and of all wisdom and science.

Mention has already been made of several well-known drugs of universal vogue that were first used by the Egyptians. Such are hartshorn, castor-oil, cumin, dill, coriander and others. But in addition to these more obvious examples, many of the drugs and their properties that occur in the works of Dioscorides, Galen, Pliny and others, were clearly borrowed from the Egyptians. These writers are the sources from which the compilers of herbals and books of popular remedies mainly drew for their information, and the works of classical authors are merely the stepping stones by which much Egyptian medical lore reached Europe. When a drug really possesses the virtues attributed to it, and is an effective remedy for disease, its survival into modern times is quite natural, but the fact that many quite fantastic remedies have been carried on almost to our own days, is definite proof of the slavish copying from the works of one writer to another in a continuous line that originated many centuries ago on the banks of the Nile. Egyptian influence can be traced in Hebrew, Persian, Syriac and Arabic medical works, and the compilers of the popular books of medicine, in spite of their oft-repeated claims to originality, are often perpetuating the use of drugs and remedies of very ancient origin.

It is from the popular writers of the seventeenth and eighteenth centuries that much of the surviving folk-medicine of western Europe is probably due, but it is likely also that many customs and beliefs had penetrated as far as the British Isles long before the invention of printing and were transmitted by the migrations and contact of peoples.

There are many reasons for believing that the works of classical writers were not the only, nor even the principal, means by which Egyptian medicine reached western Europe. Many early medical manuscripts of the thirteenth and fourteenth centuries, for instance, not only contain unmistakable Egyptian elements, but are drawn up in exactly the same manner as the ancient medical papyri. The remedies are headed by the name of the disease they were designed to cure, and each is followed by a long series of alternatives, each, as in Egypt, headed by the word 'another'. Charms and incantations are interspersed amongst the prescriptions, which are very similar to the spells in the Egyptian documents, although the names of Rē, Horus, Isis and the lesser divinities invoked are replaced by those of Christ, the Virgin and the Christian saints. At the end of the prescriptions such words are often added as 'probatum', 'tried and found perfect', etc., echoing in almost the same words the comments added to the remedies in the papyri, 'a perfect remedy', 'proved millions of times', etc. These general considerations, taken cumulatively, and in conjunction with the similar form and nature of the prescriptions, leave little doubt that the substance of the Egyptian medical books had penetrated Europe

long before the more obvious modes of communica-
tion existed.

In substantiation of what has been said, a few
examples of such transference or survival may be
cited. One of the Egyptian papyri, written about
1400 B.C., prescribes the eating of a skinned mouse
as a remedy for an infantile ailment,[1] but there is
positive evidence that the use of the mouse as a
child's medicine was many centuries older in Egypt
than this first written record of it. In a pre-dynastic
cemetery in Upper Egypt, which at the lowest possible
computation is over six thousand years old, remains
of mice were discovered in the alimentary canals of
the bodies of children under circumstances that prove
that the little animals had been skinned before they
were eaten. The mice were evidently administered
to the children as a last resource before they died.[2]
There is abundant literary evidence of the therapeutic
use of the mouse for various purposes, but usually
for children, throughout classical, medieval and later
times, and the custom of giving mice as a medicine
to children is not yet extinct in many parts of Europe
to-day. There are many persons still living in the
British Isles who in their childhood had been made
to swallow skinned mice as a remedy for whooping-
cough and other childish ailments. In April 1925,
after a lecture that I gave before the Folk-Lore
Society on mice in magic and medicine, two of my
audience told me of their experiences of mouse-eating
in childhood, and I have since come across a number

[1] *Berlin Papyrus*, 3027, 8, 2–3.
[2] G. Elliot Smith, *The Ancient Egyptians*, 2nd ed. (London
1923), p. 50.

of other cases.   This affords a striking example of the persistence of a remedy for more than sixty centuries.[1]

In two of the prescriptions of the Ebers Papyrus the spine (quill, that is to say, not backbone) of a hedgehog, calcined and beaten up with grease, is used as an ointment for alopecia.[2] Dioscorides also states that burnt hedgehogs' spines are good for alopecia,[3] and this remedy has survived in rural districts almost to the present day.

An ingredient frequently used in the remedies of the Egyptian papyri is the 'milk of a woman who has borne a male child'. This is to be found in innumerable medical works, classical, medieval and modern; whole pages would be necessary to give a collection of references.

Another instance of survival is the use of the blood of a bat as a depilatory.   It is so used in the Ebers Papyrus,[4] and in many later works of various countries. For instance, in the writings of the School of Salerno the following is to be found :

> ' De pilis evulsis ne iterum crescant.
> Ne crescant iterum loca quælibet unge pilorum
> Verbenæ succo mixto vespertilionis
> Sanguine.' [5]

---

[1] I have collected a large amount of literary evidence of the therapeutic use of mice from ancient to modern times in the *Journal of Egyptian Archæology*, Vol. x (1924), pp. 83–86, in the *American Druggist*, February 1926, and in *Folk-Lore*, Vol. xxxvi (1925), pp. 227–248.

[2] *Ebers Papyrus*, 66, 12–13 ; 92, 7–8.

[3] *De Materia Medica*, ii, 2.

[4] *Ebers*, 63, 12, 13, 18.

[5] S. de Renzi, *Collectio Salernitana*, Vol. iv (Naples 1856), p. 28.

It is interesting to note in this connection that another uncouth but common medicament in the medieval and late medical works—the blood of bugs—can be traced to the same source owing to the confusion of the superficially similar Egyptian words for ' bug ' and ' bat '.

One of the most striking instances of survival is the case of certain measures to be taken to ascertain whether a woman is pregnant or not, sterile or fertile, and the sex of unborn children. As early as the Twelfth Dynasty such nostrums are found in the Kahun Medical Papyrus. A similar collection is written on the back of the Berlin Medical Papyrus, and there is an analogous passage in the London-Leiden Magical Papyrus. In the Berlin Papyrus is the following entry :

' To know a woman who will bear from a woman who will not bear. Water-melon, pounded and bottled with the milk of a woman who has borne a male child : make it into a dose. To be swallowed by the woman. If she vomits, she will bear : if she has eructations, she will never bear.' [1]

This passage is of particular interest, because it has survived, with little alteration, in Greek medicine. In the work *Concerning the Sterile* of the Hippocratic collection,[2] the following will be found :

' If you wish to know if a woman will become pregnant, give her to swallow *butyron* (βούτυρον) and the milk of a woman who has borne a male child. If she has eructations, then she will conceive, but if not, then she will not.'

---

[1] *Berlin Medical Papyrus*, Verso, I, 3–4.

[2] Cap. vi. This book is not generally accepted as a genuine Hippocratic work. The question of authorship, however, does not now concern us.

This translation is from my copy of Hippocrates, which is that of Van der Linden, published in Leiden in 1665. In Littré's great edition of Hippocrates, a similar, but not identical, text is given.[1] In Kuhn's edition another variant text is to be found, where instead of βούτυρον simply, we have σικύην ἤ βούτυρον, ' cucumber or *butyron* '.[2] This is important, because it shows that *butyron* is not ' butter ', as most editors have rendered it, but a fruit in parallelism with cucumber. Theophrastus does not mention βούτυρον, but we know from Herychius, Athenæus and others that there was a plant so called, and it has evidently a large juicy fruit, since Kuhn's text gives it as an alternative for cucumber.[3] The Egyptian word for water-melon, that occurs in the Berlin Papyrus quoted above and elsewhere is *bdd*, or *bddw* (the consonants only are written in Egyptian), and it seems evident that when the prescription was borrowed by the Greeks, they adopted their similarly-sounding word βούτυρον as the equivalent of the Egyptian *bdd*, which represents the same or a similar fruit.

The Berlin Papyrus has also a variant form of the same recipe.

' Another prescription. Water-melon bottled with the milk of a woman who has borne a male child. Insert it into her vulva. If she vomits, she will bear : if she has eructations, she will not bear.'[4]

---

[1] E. Littré, *Œuvres Complètes d'Hippocrate* (Paris 1839–1861), t. viii, p. 415.

[2] *Magni Hippocratis Opera Omnia* (Leipsic 1825), Vol. iii, p. 6.

[3] P. le P. Renouf, *Zeitschrift für ägyptische Sprache*, Bd. xi (1873), p. 123.   [4] *Berlin Medical Papyrus*, Verso, 1, 5–6.

This only differs from the preceding by its method of administration. The Berlin Papyrus contains some further passages relating to the same subject.

'Another test for a woman who will not bear. . . . She is to be fumigated with hippopotamus dung. If she urinates, or evacuates, or passes wind at the same moment, she will bear; but if not, she will not bear. . .' [1]

The first and last words of this passage are unintelligible, and I have therefore omitted them.

'Another test. Let her go to bed after thou hast anointed her nipples, her arms, and her shoulders with fresh grease. In the morning thou shalt examine her. If thou findest her flesh light green, without being moist—she will bear normally. If thou findest it moist like the skin of [the rest of] her flesh—it is uncertain. But if thou findest it dark green when thou examinest her,—she will bear with difficulty.' [2]

The Kahun Papyrus has a passage concerning the ascertainment of pregnancy in which the expression occurs, 'if thou seest her face green ',[3] and another in which the moisture of the flesh is mentioned. Both this and the Berlin passage above are very obscure, but they are of great interest in connection with the belief, that still persists, in a greenish flesh-tint as a sign of pregnancy.[4]

[1] *Berlin Medical Papyrus*, Verso, 1, 7–8.

[2] *Ibid.*, Verso, 1, 9–11. This passage, like the others, is corrupt and difficult. The translation is only approximate, but the sense, which is all that now concerns us, is quite clear.

[3] *Kahun Medical Papyrus*, 3, 24. There are seventeen fragmentary passages relating to pregnancy and its signs in this manuscript.

[4] See the instances mentioned by Dr. D. Rorie, *Caledonian Medical Journal*, Vol. xiii (Glasgow 1926), p. 91.

'Another test. Grasp her fingers in thy hand, and grip her arm. [What follows is obscure, but the concluding sentence makes it clear that pregnancy can be ascertained by pulsation.] 'If the veins within her arm beat against thy hand, thou shalt say: "She will become pregnant"'.[1]

'Another test, whereby thou shalt ascertain. Place her in the doorway, and if thou findest the appearance of her eyes, the one like that of an Asiatic, the other like that of a negress, then she will not bear. If thou findest colour in one of them, then she will bear.'[2]

Presumably the object of taking the woman to the doorway was to place her in a good light in order to examine the appearance of her eyes, although it is not at all clear what the expected appearance would be like. We now come to the most remarkable in the whole collection, because it has survived to the present day.

'Another test for a woman who will bear or a woman who will not bear. Wheat and spelt: let the woman water them daily with her urine, like dates and like sh'at-seeds in two bags. If they both grow, she will bear: if the wheat grows it will be a boy; if the spelt grows, it will be a girl. If neither grows, she will not bear.'[3]

The earliest variant of this passage occurs in the London-Leiden Magical Papyrus, and reads thus:

'The way to know it of a woman whether she is enceinte: you make a woman pass her water on this herb as above again in the evening; when the morning comes, and if you find the plant scorched (?), she will not conceive; if you find it flourishing, she will conceive.'[4]

---

[1] *Berlin Medical Papyrus*, Verso, 1, 11–13.
[2] *Ibid.*, Verso, 2, 1–2.   [3] *Ibid.*, Verso, 2, 2–5.
[4] Verso, 5, 4–8; Griffith and Thompson, *The Demotic Magical Papyrus*, Vol. i (London 1904), p. 177.

Variants of this experiment occur not infrequently in old books of household and medical recipes. The following three variants are quoted from a work entitled *The Experienced Midwife,* a book that has enjoyed great popularity and that has been reprinted in edition after edition from the end of the seventeenth century to the present day. It is included in a collection that is sold to-day under the ludicrous title *The Works of Aristotle, the Famous Philosopher.* The three variants are as follows :—

(i) ' To know whether the fault [sterility] is in the man or the woman, sprinkle the man's urine upon a lettuce leaf, and the woman's upon another, and that which dies away first is unfruitful.'

(ii) ' And take five wheaten corns and seven beans, put them into an earthen pot, and let the party make water therein ; let this stand seven days, and if in that time they begin to sprout, then the party is fruitful ; but if they sprout not, then the party is barren, whether it be the man or the woman ; this is a certain sign.'

(iii) ' Culpeper and others also give a great deal of credit to the following experiment. Take a handful of barley, and steep half of it in the urine of a man, and the other half in the urine of a woman, for the space of twenty-four hours ; then take it out, and put the man's by itself ; set it in a flower-pot, or some other thing, where let it dry ; water the man's every morning with his own urine, and the woman's with hers, and that which grows first is the most fruitful ; but if they grow not at all, they are both naturally barren.'

Although the last of the above three experiments is attributed to Culpeper, his version differs considerably.

' To know if a woman be with child. If a woman desire to know whether she be with Child or not, let her make water in a clean Copper or Brazen Vessel at night when she goes to bed, and put a Nettle into it ; if the Nettle have red spots in it in the next morning, she is with Child, else not.' [1]

For comparison, I will give two further versions of the experiment, one of the seventeenth, the other of the eighteenth century :

' If ye be desirous to know whether the man or the woman be hindrance in conception, let each of them take wheat and barley corns, and of beans, of each 7, the which they shall suffer to be steeped in their several urine the space of twentie and foure houres ; then take two pots such as they set Gelli-flowers in, fill them with good earth, and in the one, let be set the Wheat, Barley and Beans steeped in the man's water, and in the other Wheat, Barley and Beans steeped in the woman's water, and every morning the space of eight or ten dayes, let each of them with their proper urine water the said seeds sown in the foresaid pots, and mark whose pots doth prove and the seeds therein contained doth grow, and that party is not the lack of conception, and see that there come no other water or rain on the pots, but trust not much this far fetcht experiment.' [2]

' Make two holes in the ground : throw barley into one and wheat into the other, then pour into both the water of the pregnant woman and cover them up again with earth. If the wheat sprouts before the barley, it will be a boy ; if the barley comes up first, thou must expect a daughter.'

I have given all these ridiculous and unsavoury experiments at length, because they afford a very

---

[1] *Culpeper's Last Legacy* (London 1671), p. 269.
[2] Reynald, *Birth of Mankind*, 3rd ed. (London 1654), p. 188. This extract was sent to me by a correspondent : I have not seen the book. The next quotation, by one Peter Bayer, was also sent by a correspondent, but without reference.

good instance of the persistence in popular medicine of ancient magical beliefs. Their age exceeds three thousand years from the time of the Berlin Papyrus, and the fragments in the Kahun Papyrus take them back another millennium. Many other instances might be quoted of the survival of ancient medical and magical ideas, but one further ancient belief must suffice.

When speaking of Assyrian medicine, mention was made of the belief, also current in Egypt, that dental disease is caused by worms. This belief is widespread to-day : it is found in Western Asia, in China, in the Malay Peninsula and in many other places, and it was current in Europe a century ago. Remedies for worms in the teeth are common in old medical books, and as an example, the following recipe from a fourteenth-century manuscript may be quoted :

'For toth-ache of wurmes. Take hennebane-seede and leke-seed and poudre of encens, of iche Ilike mychil, and ley hem on a tyl-ston hot glowyng and make a pipe of latoun [latten] that the nether ende de wyde that it may ouer-closen the sedes and the poudre and hald his mouth there ouer the ouerende that the eyre may in-to the sore tothe and that wil slew the wurmes and do away the ache.' [1]

Reference has already been made to the fact that the oft-repeated statement that the mandrake was used by the Egyptians in medicine is entirely without foundation (see above, p. 113). The Assyrians, however, knew the plant and used it frequently in their

[1] G. Henslow, *Medical Works of the Fourteenth Century* (London 1899), p. 95. It is interesting to note that incense mixed with vegetable drugs is used in several of the prescriptions for the teeth in the Ebers Papyrus.

11

prescriptions. Dr. Campbell Thompson has shown that our word 'mandrake' is merely the Assyrian word 'Plague-god-plant' slightly changed by the merchants who introduced the word into Europe as the Greek *mandragora*, which is derived from the Assyrian name *nam-ta-ira* by the simple metathesis of the letters *m* and *n*. He has also shown that the Greek word *sukaminos* is similarly derived from the Assyrian name of the mulberry, *musakanu*; by transposing the first two consonants, the Greek name, for which there has hitherto been no satisfactory etymology, was thus brought with the tree from the East.[1]

In Egypt and Assyria medical science had its beginnings. It has been shown that on the banks of the Nile more than three thousand years before the Christian Era a definite attempt was being made to cope with the problems of life and death. The driving motive out of which the science of medicine has evolved was the endeavour to prolong and protect life and to avert extinction. The arts of both the embalmer and the physician were concerned with devising the means of protecting the individual against the dangers that threatened his existence when alive and his continued existence after death. These dangers were for the most part supernatural and beyond man's finite comprehension. The magical procedures used in both cases had a single object in view—the giving of life that death and disease had stolen or threatened. The embalmer by his manipulations contrived to preserve the physical frame of the body, and the magician infused into it the vital

[1] *The Assyrian Herbal* (London 1924), pp. 189, 190.

substance that was hostile to the demons of destruction and essential to the continuance of existence.

The peculiar circumstances arising out of Egyptian customs and beliefs provided the facilities that made real medical research possible, facilities that were unattainable everywhere else. The Greek anatomists, as mentioned in Chapter VI, were able to practise the dissection of the human body in Egypt in the third century B.C., and the medical papyri show that the Egyptians themselves in far earlier times had some knowledge of the structure and functions of the human frame that the Greeks for many centuries had lacked. If Egypt cannot compete with Greece in scientific medical knowledge and thought, she at least inaugurated what others have developed and led the way to facilities for the advancement of knowledge and research that could not otherwise have existed.

INDEX

151

Printed in the USA
CPSIA information can be obtained
at www.ICGtesting.com
LVHW071630100124
768361LV00055B/1506